McCor

Mark H. McCormack was an associate at a
Cleveland law firm when, following a
lifelong passion for golf, he began to represent a young unknown called Arnold
Palmer. A host of sports celebrities in golf,
tennis and other areas followed, as did
wide diversification. McCormack's
innovations in merchandising, licensing
and television programming are credited as
the single most important influence in the
transformation of sports into big business.

In America, McCormack has been listed as
'The most powerful man in sports', and in
Great Britain the *Sunday Times* chose him
as one of the 1,000 people who have most
influenced the twentieth century. The firm
he founded, International Management
Group (IMG), now has 67 offices in 26
countries and employs nearly 2,000 people.
IMG represents many organizations
diverse as Wi
Foundation
McCormack
bestsellers in
You at Harva

Also by Mark McCormack

McCormack on Negotiating
McCormack on Managing
McCormack on Communicating

BOOKS SHOULD BE RETURNED ON OR BEFORE THE LAST DATE
SHOWN BELOW. BOOKS NOT ALREADY REQUESTED BY OTHER
READERS MAY BE RENEWED BY PERSONAL APPLICATION, BY
WRITING, OR BY TELEPHONE. TO RENEW, GIVE THE DATE DUE
AND THE NUMBER ON THE BARCODE LABEL.

FINES CHARGED FOR OVERDUE BOOKS WILL INCLUDE POSTAGE
INCURRED IN RECOVERY. DAMAGE TO, OR LOSS OF, BOOKS
WILL BE CHARGED TO THE BORROWER.

Arrow Books Limited 1996

10 9 8 7 6 5 4 3 2 1

Arrow Books Limited
20 Vauxhall Bridge Road, London SW1V 2SA

Random House Australia (Pty) Limited
20 Alfred Street, Milsons Point, Sydney
New South Wales 2061, Australia

Random House New Zealand Limited
18 Poland Road, Glenfield
Auckland 10, New Zealand

Random House South Africa (Pty) Limited
PO Box 337, Bergvlei, South Africa

Papers used by Random House UK Limited
are natural, recyclable products made from wood grown in
sustainable forests. The manufacturing processes conform to
the environmental regulations of the country of origin.

Companies, institutions and other organizations wishing to make
bulk purchases of any business books published by Random House
should contact their local bookstore or Random House direct:
Special Sales Director
Random House
20 Vauxhall Bridge Road
London SW1V 2SA
Tel: 0171 973 9670   Fax: 0171 828 6681

Random House UK Limited Reg. No. 954009

ISBN 0 09 953651 X

Printed and bound in Great Britain by
Cox & Wyman Ltd, Reading, Berkshire

Contents

Introduction
There Are No Fads in Selling

Of all the phenomenal developments during my 35 years in business, none is more curious to me than the massive proliferation of management theories (or to be less charitable, business fads). I first started paying attention to this phenomenon in the early 1980s when *excellence* was all the rage and the business press urged all managers to emulate a handful of demonstrably 'excellent' companies. A year or two later the new mantra was *corporate culture*. Then it was *quality*, only to be superseded by *leadership* and *competitive advantage* and *empowerment* and *being true to the customer*. (This is not a complete list.) As I write this, the theory du jour seems to be *re-engineering* (which contends that managers must constantly adapt and transform their organizations to constant and rapid change).

It's hard to argue with any of these theories, especially when you consider the alternatives to 'excellence' and 'quality'. But it's always fascinated me that, in the midst of this epidemic of management fads, no one has come up with an equivalent system or catch-all phrase for the most important activity in business – namely, selling.

I think I know why. Management concepts and techniques adapt to changes in the social, political, and financial landscape. We seem to demand a steady supply of quick-fix theories and gimmicks to help us cope with steady change.

Selling, on the other hand, never changes. It has always been – and always will be – a simple three-step process of:

- Identify the customer.
- Reach the customer.
- Persuade the customer to buy.

If you sell for a living, you know this is the blunt unwavering formula for success. At any point in the sales process, if you're not doing one of these three things, you're not selling. That's why there are no fads in selling. No matter what the changes in the social or political fabric of an economy, selling has remained remarkably the same in its purpose (generate revenue) and its method (identify, reach, persuade).

No change, no theories or fads needed.

I suppose you could argue that there have been major advances in the tools that salespeople use today. Computerized databases now let you identify customers you never knew existed twenty years ago. Cellular phones now mean that you can reach anyone anytime. Elements of show business – from multimedia presentations to video proposals – can now be employed to supercharge your powers of persuasion in front of the customer.

But these are just technical improvements – like giving a long-distance runner a pair of 'new and improved' track shoes. The shoes may be lighter and more comfortable. They may even help an athlete run a fraction faster. But they don't change the basics of running. The athlete still has to put one foot in front of the other as fast as he can.

It's no different with selling. Whether you're the type of salesperson who cannot live without the latest gadgetry (the cellular phone that weighs a half-ounce less, the palm-size computer with twice the memory, the fax machine in the car) or you can function happily with a legal pad and a handful of index cards (that's me), the tools don't change the fact that, at some point, you have to ask for the order and persuade the customer to commit.

I emphasize this point at the start because I don't pretend to have a unified theory of selling. If you're looking for catchy phrases and inspirational mottoes that will miraculously spur you to greater sales glory, you won't find them here.

This book starts and finishes with the premise that selling is an understanding of people and the judicious application of common sense. This book assumes that all of us are born salespeople. When we persuade our peers at school to accept us or our parents to let us stay out late or an employer to hire us, we are selling. This book also assumes that, for many of us, life and work represents a gradual erosion of these innate selling skills. This book is an attempt to help people recapture those skills – by helping them simplify rather than overcomplicate the selling process, by teaching them how to avoid making errors in the marketplace that they would never make in their personal life, by introducing them to a salesperson's three biggest obstacles (namely, fear, ignorance, and sloth), and by getting them to think more about the customer and what they're selling and less about themselves.

On a sales call this would be the point where I would present my credentials. After all, who am I to teach and preach successful selling?

My principle sales credential is that I run a sports marketing company, which I started 35 years ago in Cleveland, Ohio, with $500 in capital, called International Management Group, or simply IMG.

We represent hundreds of well-known athletes such as

Arnold Palmer (my first client), Jackie Stewart, Jean-Claude Killy, Bjorn Borg, Martina Navratilova, Alberto Tomba, and Andre Agassi. In recent years, we have branched out into the representation of classical musicians and singers such as Itzhak Perlman, James Galway, and Sir Neville Marriner.

We create and manage events, everything from the World Match Play at Wentworth to a José Carreras concert in Singapore to the Detroit Grand Prix motor race to 'Jesus Christ Superstar' in Sydney to the Dubai Snooker Classic.

We represent the Nobel Foundation. We have helped develop the commercial interests of Wimbledon and the Royal and Ancient Golf Club of St. Andrews.

Our television arm, Trans World International, has represented the international broadcast rights for sports properties such as the Olympic Games, the World and European Figure Skating championships, the National Football League, all the major golf and tennis championships, and the 24 Hours of Le Mans. It is also the world's largest independent producer of television sports programming.

Although I started out as a lawyer at a large established law firm, I realized quickly when I went out on my own that, if I wanted to stay in business, I would have to start thinking of myself as a salesman first and a lawyer second. In the course of 35 years at the helm of IMG, I have sold virtually every feature and benefit associated with sport – from an athlete's name and personal services to a sponsor's banner at a figure skating show to the television rights to a golf tournament – on every continent.

I have sold things that people never thought were 'for sale'. The sleeves of tennis players were commercial-free until our company pointed out to advertisers that a top-ranked tennis player's shoulder appears on television hundreds of times during a championship match. With all that generous exposure on national television, wouldn't that be a great place for a company to place its logo? Our company made the sleeves available and, thus, the first 'patch deal' was sold.

In 1984 when I wrote my first book, *What They Don't Teach You at Harvard Business School*, IMG had 500 employees in 19 offices around the world generating several hundred million dollars in revenue. Today, we have nearly 2000 employees and 67 offices in 26 countries and revenues have surged well beyond the billion-dollar mark. We have obviously continued selling in the interval.

Before writing *On Selling* I got to know the competition. All the books on the subject took the commendable position that selling is *the single-most important activity in business*. I applaud that. As the saying goes, nothing happens until someone sells something. But, to my mind, the majority of them misplaced their focus. They had far too much emphasis on improving *you*.

They had rules on how you should dress (as if selecting the proper necktie spelled the difference between a yes and a no).

They had lists of what you should say in 'the 24 most common selling situations' (as if every customer fell neatly into one of 24 categories and that closing the deal only required you to spout the corresponding bromide or cliché).

They had suggestions on how you should enter the room, shake hands, sit down, talk, listen, shift in your chair, move your hands, modulate your voice, make eye contact, apply persuasive body language, etc. (as if remodeling you could dramatically change your customers' need for your product or service).

I would have been more intrigued if the books had shifted the emphasis onto the customer and the product or service being sold – because that's the way I've been selling for 35 years.

Most disturbing, though, was the fact that many of the books were written by people who had never actually sold something for a living. Their advice revolved around hypothetical examples or retellings of spectacular deals clipped from magazines and newspapers.

The selling examples you'll read here have involved me or our company in some way. In other words, they're real. In some cases, we look brilliant, in others not so brilliant. I cite the triumphs so you can understand the inner workings of a successful sale. I cite the disasters so you don't repeat my mistakes.

Before we start, I want to explain the difference between *negotiating* and *selling*. As any salesperson knows, there's an extremely fine line between selling and negotiating. Sometimes there is no line at all. You are trying to generate interest in your product or service at the same time that you are going back and forth with the customer about the best price. The customer is intrigued at one price, indifferent at another. How do you define the give and take over price? Is it selling or negotiating? It's hard to say. For the purposes of this primer, let us agree that selling is the process of identifying customers, getting through to them, increasing their awareness and interest in your product or service, and finally persuading them to act on that interest. Let us also agree that negotiating is the end game of the sales process in which your objective is to secure the best terms once the other side starts to act on their interest. (I cover this in a companion volume, *On Negotiating*.)

With that caveat in mind, let's get started.

Chapter 1
How Anyone Can Make Me Buy

Over the course of this book, you will be relentlessly exposed to the qualities that I believe make a good salesman.

- Believe in your product.
- Believe in yourself.
- See a lot of people.
- Pay attention to timing.
- Listen to the customer (but realize that what the customer wants is not necessarily what he or she is telling you).
- Develop a sense of humor.
- Knock on old doors.
- Ask everyone to buy.
- Follow up after the sale with the same aggressiveness you demonstrated before the sale.
- Use common sense.

I have no illusions that I'm breaking new ground with this list. These are essential, self-evident, universal qualities that all salespeople know in their heads (if not their hearts).

What's interesting to me, however, is how little impact these prized attributes would have on me. Going through the list, I see only two qualities that could persuade me to buy.

Take the first two items. I'm sufficiently insulated at our company nowadays that I don't have to see salespeople off the street. I can be selective. The salespeople I meet tend to have their bona fides in order and a legitimate reason to see me. As a result, I rarely meet salespeople who do *not* believe in their product or themselves. But confidence alone won't close a sale with me. At best, it simply won't undo a sale.

Likewise with salespeople who make a point of seeing a lot of prospects. Like most people, I don't like the feeling that I'm just a name and number on someone's massive checklist of 'People to Call'. It might be an essential step in defining your customer base, but it's not how I define myself. Lump me in a crowd and you won't get my money. Make me feel unique, as if I'm the first person you ever called on with your product or service, and you will.

Paying attention to timing also won't work with me. No matter how carefully you calibrate the perfect moment to ask for my order, I pride myself on keeping my buying timetable to myself and sticking to it. Unless you know my timetable, you can't make me buy.

The same with asking for the order, following up aggressively, and knocking on old doors (i.e., selling to people who have bought from you before). These are absolute-must sales devices, but I've been in the selling arena long enough to resist their blunt charms.

As for listening to the customer, I respect the concept so much it's my first weapon of choice too (whether I'm selling or buying). In any transaction, I'd rather start out by getting information than giving it away. If listening is your favorite tool, we cancel each other out.

One attribute that does have a persuasive impact, though, is a sense of humor. I'm not suggesting that I open up my wallet to anyone who can tell a joke. But people who can maintain a sense of humor about their job, their goals, and themselves tend to put me at ease. I like being around them, even when I know they are trying to sell me something. Because of that comfort zone, I don't have a problem telling them no when their idea is wrong for me and, conversely, I don't put up as many barriers to saying yes when their idea is right (or almost right) for me. Their sense of humor makes it easier for me to buy.

The other attribute that works on me, of course, is common sense. Common sense will tell you to step back and look at my business. What does our company do? Who do we deal with? Who have we bought from in the past? How have we grown? What do we need?

Common sense will tell you to talk to people who know me. You'll learn who I admire and what kind of logic I respect. You'll learn that, like anyone else, I have emotional and intellectual hot buttons worth pushing. You'll learn that I have tendencies and response patterns of which I am unaware that amuse my friends and associates and could give you a slight edge in dealing with me.

Common sense will even tell you to read my books. If you were calling on a decision maker at any company, public or private, you'd surely prepare by reading a few newspaper and magazine clippings on the company or peruse an annual report or two. This is really basic research, the rawest form of due diligence. Well, I've made it easy for salespeople who want my money. Over the last ten years I've written a handful of books and published a monthly newsletter that literally tells people, warts and all, our company's basic philosophy and our favorite tactics and strategies. Yet I cannot count the number of times people have walked into my office, pitched me their product or service, and in the course of our meeting revealed somehow that they've never read a single word

I've written or, in truly disheartening instances, have even been unaware of my books. It's not the discourtesy or the ego deflation that turns me off; it's their lack of preparation. If they overlook this obvious fact about me, what else will they miss when we start doing business together?

Common sense will also tell you to keep reading, because the following tactics really work with me.

1   Tell me it's the best.

If I have a core business philosophy, it is this: 'Work with the best.' I stumbled on this representing my first three clients – Palmer, Player, and Nicklaus – which taught me indelibly how much easier it was to sell the services of the number one, two, and three golfers in the world than the 101st, 102nd, and 103rd golfers. We extended that 'work with the best' philosophy to everything we tried. When we got involved in winter sports, our first client was triple-gold-medalist Jean-Claude Killy. When we entered the tennis arena, our first client was Grand Slam champion Rod Laver. In motor sports, it was Formula I world champion Jackie Stewart. When we got involved with tennis events, our first account was Wimbledon. When we started advising non-sports institutions, we began with the Nobel Foundation. Whether it was athletes, events, or institutions, we regarded each not only as 'best of breed' but leap years ahead of the nearest competitor. This wasn't snobbery or arrogance on our part. It was good business. Selling the best is fun (and extremely profitable). Selling also-rans is hard work (and marginally profitable at best).

That thinking pervades my buying habits as well. Frankly, I'm a sucker for the best. If you can convince me that the car you're selling is a Lexus, the watch a Rolex, the suit from Alfred Dunhill, the pen a Montblanc, etc. (the brand names vary according to personal taste), you can make me buy.

2   Outwait me.

I hate to be rushed. I don't like people telling me, 'I need your answer by the close of business tomorrow,' or 'This offer is good for one day only,' or 'This is the last unit we have,' or any other variation that forces me to make a snap decision. I have my own timetable and I'm willing to wait. I also turn extremely skeptical when the rush is on. I'll wait a week to see if you've extended your 'one day sale' or still have that 'last unit' in stock. If you're willing to wait for me, you can make me buy.

3   Reach me through my family.

One of the niftiest sales I ever made was to the CEO of a mid-size American package goods company. In the course of a friendly first meeting in which he rejected everything I proposed, he mentioned that his daughter was attending Tulane University in New Orleans. A few months later, when we happened to be staging a Bjorn Borg tennis exhibition in New Orleans, I sent him four tickets to the match, in case his daughter and her friends wanted to see Borg play.

Two years later, when this CEO finally agreed to sponsor one of our projects, he told me the Borg tickets had made the difference. The fact that I remembered the tiny detail of Tulane University said something nice about me and our company. The fact that it was *his* daughter said something even nicer to him.

I'm not immune to that approach either. All things being equal, I am more likely to listen to your pitch if you can get my wife or children to act as your go-between. In fact, all things not being equal, if my wife or children are involved, I will still hear you out. That's human nature. Blood is thicker than water.

After that, you're on your own. Playing the family card won't persuade me to buy a bad idea or, for that matter, a semi-decent one. In fact, I usually seek a second opinion in these situations. If you can convince one other disinterested party at our company to buy into your concept, you have me on your side.

4   See the small picture.

In other words, think small before you think big.

I've been telling our sales executives for years not to automatically equate the size of their proposal with the size of the company. People see a huge corporation such as Philip Morris or General Motors and they think that only a huge proposal with huge numbers will catch the company's attention. Actually, when you consider how many overpriced proposals giant corporations have seen over the years as a result of this thinking, the opposite is true. A smaller proposal will be infinitely more interesting.

In the last decade, our company has quadrupled in size. Outside salespeople now consider us 'big' – and the concepts they're pitching us have grown bigger too. The fact is that we are not a monolithic structure with one large pot of money to dispense to the right seller. We're more like a union of four dozen profit centers in 26 countries, each with its own budget and profit goals. A salesperson who pays attention to this fact, who sees the small picture and tailors his sales pitch to the appropriate profit center at our company rather than the company itself stands a much better chance of getting me to buy.

5 Save me money.

Some efficiency-minded people will spend money on any gadget or service that saves them time. Some hedonistic types will invest in anything that increases their creature comforts. Then there are gamblers who plunge into anything that has a 50/50 chance of hitting the jackpot.

Personally, I'm always looking to save money. I'm hardly unique in abhorring excess, but there are not as many of me in the business world as you may think. Given the choice between selling me a concept that (a) *may* make me money and (b) represents a cheaper way of doing business, you will do better with the latter.

6 Be my friend.

I have a sentimental streak that sometimes compels me to say yes when logic and simple arithmetic are screaming at me to say no. I know chief executives who have held onto veteran employees long after their usefulness to the company had passed simply because the employees' loyalty to the company outweighed their productivity on the job. Sentiment triumphed over reason.

The same impulse afflicts me as a buyer sometimes. If you are a trusted friend who needs my patronage to help you out of a cash-flow crisis, I'm a good prospect even when I don't really need what you are selling. If you don't make a habit of it, you can always make me buy.

7   Cater to my *personal* agenda.

Customers' buying habits are a reflection of either a corporate agenda, a personal agenda, or a combination of both.

For example, in the early 1960s, which I consider the infant days of sports marketing, when we sold a golf concept to a corporate sponsor, it was usually because the company's CEO loved golf (and we knew it). The sale fitted in with the CEO's personal agenda. Our company hadn't been around long enough to prove that golf could help achieve a company's business objectives – that is, its corporate agenda. That came later. Nowadays, marketing via sports is fairly sophisticated. You have to focus exclusively on the corporate agenda. No matter how passionate a decision maker may be about golf, you won't make the sale unless you demonstrate that golf is an effective way to reach that buyer's target audience. Our salespeople are keenly aware of the difference between corporate and personal agendas – and sell accordingly.

A similar appreciation would work with me.

In most people's minds, I am the CEO of IMG. So when they're trying to sell me something, they usually appeal to my sense of the company's needs. That's smart. As IMG's ultimate decision maker, I am presumably the guardian of our corporate agenda. Appeal to that and you appeal to me. The reality, though, is that I rarely make a unilateral buying decision. I review it first with our senior managers to make sure *they* think it fits in with our corporate agenda. In other words, salespeople aren't talking to me, they're talking to a committee.

But I do have a life as a 'private citizen' beyond my company role. For one thing, as an author, I'm a client of our company. IMG negotiates my book contracts, speaking fees, newspaper columns, and television appearances – and like any other client, I pay the standard commission. A lot of people have a tough time separating my CEO role from my client role. But those who can soon find out that I have different buying habits in the latter role. As a client, I make unilateral decisions and pursue a personal agenda. Approach me that way, and you can make me buy.

I remember 10 years ago, after my first book became a best seller, an American publisher suggested I write a monthly newsletter on similar business themes. I would write the text. The publisher would do everything else. Design it. Print it. Market it. Mail it. Solicit subscribers. Bill them. And make sure they paid. I would pay the publisher a monthly fee for doing all these tasks and we would split the profits.

Now, this is precisely the sort of deal that I would *never* take to another IMG client. It's not our job to create business opportunities in which our clients pay someone else or invest their money on a risky proposition. (Clients don't need us to help them toss their money away.) Our job is to find opportunities where our clients get paid for their time and talent. That has always been our corporate agenda.

In ordinary circumstances, the people representing me would insist on a financial guarantee for me or that the publisher assume all the risk. But the publisher was shrewd about the distinction between my corporate and personal agendas. He somehow knew he was talking to me strictly as a client – and that I bought differently in that role. He appealed to my entepreneurial instincts, my willingness to take a flyer with my money, and yes, my personal vanity (the newsletter would have my name on it, not IMG's). So I bought into the concept, even though it went against everything our company preaches. (A decade later, with the newsletter still rolling along, I'm glad I did.)

If you can separate my personal agenda from my corporate agenda, you can make me buy.

Chapter 2
The Components of Common Sense

At almost every speech someone in the audience asks me whether I worry about giving away too many of my business secrets in the books and articles I write.

'Don't you think you're telling people how to outsmart you?' they ask.

I always reply by pointing out that just because Jack Nicklaus writes a book on how to play golf doesn't mean that everyone who reads it is going to start beating Jack Nicklaus at golf.

There's a touch of arrogance in that remark, but the cold hard truth is that very few people have Jack Nicklaus's talent, power, physical coordination, technical mastery, composure, and confidence. An even colder truth: of the few who approximate this skill set, fewer still would have the discipline and mental toughness to maximize it.

It's not much different in business and sales. No matter how much training you give your sales force via books, tapes and seminars, there will always be a percentage of salespeople who don't learn what you want them to learn.

I'm not sure why. Perhaps they are not smart enough (the message doesn't get through). Or they're not paying attention (the message sails over their heads). Or they don't have the discipline to practice what you preach (the message gets in but not out).

But I also suspect that there are some fundamental business skills that, are, more or less, unteachable.

For example, all good salespeople need a *keen sense of timing*, knowing when to pounce on a customer and when to hold back. But I'm not sure how easily taught that skill is. I've known too many salespeople who, even if I supplied them with a minute-by-minute timetable on how to approach a customer, would find a way to misread the timetable or the customer's cues.

Likewise, the best salespeople know *how to handle rejection*. They expect to hear 'no' more often than 'yes' in their line of work. So they start out with thick skin, and it gets thicker with the years. But again, I'm not sure you can teach thick skin. Like *speed* in sports (where every coach loves fast athletes because 'you can't teach speed'), you have to be born with it.

The best salespeople also have *personal charm*. They may not be liked by everyone, but they have an instinct for getting some people (usually customers) to like them. They know that selling is, first and foremost, a seduction process, in which creating a bond of friendship and trust can affect the outcome more than the merits of the product or service being sold. Once again, I'm not convinced you can teach people to be likeable. For years I've told our salespeople, 'All things being equal, people prefer to do business with a friend. In fact, all things not being equal, people still prefer doing business with a friend.' Yet the message doesn't always sink in. People still try to rush the sale process, pushing for decisions before they have gained the customer's affection and trust.

Some people would argue that the most unteachable skill of all is *common sense*. I can see why. We all know people who have it. We all know people who lack it. We all know how wide the gap is between the two and how infrequently people bridge the gap.

It doesn't have to be that way. In my mind, common sense is unteachable only in the sense that it isn't learned overnight. A fool doesn't wake up the next morning a sage. But even the most foolish person over time can become significantly less foolish.

The key is to break down the components of common sense into those that can be taught and those that can't, focus on the former rather than the latter, and master each one at a time.

In selling, for example, here are five skills that *can* be learned by anyone. In fact, they are so basic and doable that selling without them is not only inexcusable but suicidal.

Component 1. Know your product.

You'd think this would be obvious to everyone. Yet how many times have you walked into a store, inquired about a product, and discovered that your salesperson knew even less about it than you? What kind of impression did that make? How much did it make you want to buy from that store?

My guess is that 90 per cent of all salespeople haven't fully learned this obvious, doable, essential skill. (That's why it's common sense component 1.)

I would also guess that the top 10 per cent of any sales force perfectly mirrors the 10 per cent of people who know their product cold. I don't have data to back up this estimate. I only know that I've never bought anything from salespeople who didn't know their product and yet I

have bought things I didn't know I needed from salespeople who did.

Component 2. Talk less.

This is less obvious – largely because it goes against a
salesperson's most basic instinct, *i.e.*, the instinct to be
articulate, to demonstrate your expertise, to keep on
pitching until you hit the chord that turns the customer
around. But talking less is uncommon sense, particularly
at the start of any sale when the overriding goal is to get the
customer to like you.

If flattering the customer is the easiest way to make him
like you, then letting him talk runs a close second. And,
where overzealous flattery runs the risk of sounding
insincere, talking less is never a test of your sincerity. It
shows that you respect the customer and feel he has
something to say. I've never met anyone who thought less
of me because I let them talk.

Component 3. Know the buyer.

In other words, do your homework before you walk into
the customer's office. Actually, salespeople don't need to
learn the importance of being prepared. I'm sure they
know it.

But they do need to be taught the discipline to practise it
consistently and without exception. They can't be permit-
ted to go on sales calls thinking they can 'wing it' and that
the customer won't notice. Wing it once and pretty soon it
becomes a habit.

I know one CEO so obsessed with knowing the buyer that he won't approve the travel and entertainment (T&E) expenses of a sales call unless the salesperson has prepared a dossier on the prospect. He requires all his salespeople to send a questionnaire to the prospect *before* the initial meeting so that no salesperson will waste the prospect's time asking stupid questions.

That's superb sales management. But what sticks out in my mind is the concept of linking expenses to preparation. This CEO is living proof that preparation is common sense that any salesperson can be taught.

Component 4. Aim low.

Everyone wants to hit home runs, to close the big deals that leave their colleagues gasping. Personally, I'm in awe of people who can walk into a room, ask for a big number, and get it. Like home run power in baseball, aiming high in sales and hitting the target is a gift that can't be taught. Some people can do it, most people can't.

It's much easier to teach people to aim low on a sales call. That's not an endorsement for selling your services cheaply. It's just a reminder that a small sale is doable. A small sale is how most customers want to begin a relationship. A small sale can lead to bigger things.

The worst thing about aiming too high, though, is that customers sense you are desperate to do something heroic, and that desperation is rarely an attractive or persuasive feature. Whenever I see salespeople fall into this trap, I take them aside and bring them back to reality. I tell them that hitting a home run is a long shot, that their odds of

success increase dramatically if they expect less of themselves *and* the customer.

I don't recommend lowered expectations as an every-
day strategy for getting ahead. But setting realistic goals is
common sense that's tough to learn. Aiming low is one
way to start.

Component 5. Promise less.

I was in a luncheon meeting with several executives of
another company not long ago. The atmosphere was
pleasant and as we sipped our coffee at meal's end, we
were all in agreement that our two companies should be
working together. We weren't exactly sure what we would
be working on, but there were a number of areas worth
exploring. I told the leader from the other side that we
would need some information before we could propose
the next step. He promised he would get back to me within
two weeks with his wish-list of objectives. As a favor, he
added that he would set up a meeting for me with his
international team. He then mentioned that it might be
mutually beneficial if he introduced our company to one
or two of his main corporate partners. But then he did
something extraordinary. He stopped himself and said,
'Wait a minute. I'd better not promise more than I can
deliver. Why don't I get you that list, Mark, and let's take it
from there.'

What makes that statement so extraordinary is how few
salespeople have the sense to make it. At the start of any
potentially great relationship, it's easy to get swept away
and promise more than you can possibly deliver. What
people forget is that when they leave that meeting, they

have other relationships and other promises to live up to. The promises pile up, something inevitably falls through the cracks, and without too much effort, their credibility takes a beating at the precise moment it should be soaring.

The correct course of action, which anyone can learn, is *promise less*. No one will think less of you for it.

Chapter 3
Getting the Customers You Deserve

In sales, you get the customers you deserve. If you don't believe this, just look at your company's top producers. Who do they sell to? Who are their prospects? How in terms of power, friendship, integrity, and decisiveness do their customers stack up against yours?

If you want to be a better salesperson, you should seek out better customers.

In my experience, the perfect customer is a friend who is a decision-maker who not only likes what I'm proposing but will help me conquer any pockets of resistance within his or her company.

The not-so-perfect customer is someone who says yes, lets me work my way through his company, and then gets talked out of it by subordinates. The least perfect customer, of course, is the one who doesn't agree with me in the first place.

My idea of the perfect customer may not be the same as yours nor should it be. But many people wouldn't know the perfect customer if he was sitting in front of them saying yes to everything. Here are some other qualities that can help you better identify the perfect customer when you meet him.

1   He talks. You listen.

The more you know someone, the more they will talk meaningfully to you about their problems and how they relate to you. If they trust you, they'll describe the conflicts they have with their boss or their colleagues in supporting a program you both want to do. And they'll wrestle through these internal conflicts *with you*. They'll include you in the solution. You'll rarely hear that except from a friend. And that's the perfect customer.

2   He needs you, and you don't abuse it.

There are not too many business relationships where you can take the extra edge and get away with it. But the perfect customer is one of those relationships. The perfect customer trusts you and expects you to display perfect judgment. Anything less can be disastrous.

We recently convinced a major American sporting event to do an expensive promotion involving souvenir programs to back up the event and their large investment. The idea appealed to us because we would make a lot of money on it. The idea appealed to the event directors because, frankly, they trusted us and would agree to anything we suggested. Unfortunately, our enthusiasm clouded our judgment. We overestimated the print run. We still made some money. But the customer lost money and now a perfect relationship is less perfect.

With the perfect customer who leaves many things up to your discretion you have to bend over backwards to be less fair to yourself.

3   He says no without stiffing you.

There are moments in business when you think more highly of the customer because of how they behaved when they told you no.

The perfect customer doesn't lead you on. If he's not interested, he makes it clear immediately. He respects your time. The perfect customer doesn't stiff you without warning. He prepares you for rejection, so you don't lose face among your superiors and peers.

In some cases, the perfect customer (for various reasons) might even help you obtain a better deal elsewhere.

There have been occasions when a long-time customer has given every indication that he is not particularly interested in my latest project. But I suspect he stayed in the bidding because it might induce one of his competitors to pay us more. That's not collusion or conspiracy. It's hardball competitiveness – because in the perfect customer's mind, the more his competitors spend on me, the less they have to spend against him.

4   He is not a pushover.

You implicitly give him your best price.

As a salesperson, you want the perfect customer to remain the perfect customer, i.e., come back for second and third sales. You certainly don't want to put him out of business with outrageous prices.

Conversely, the perfect customer understands your need to make a profit. While he may not be a pushover for every scheme you put on his desk, he also doesn't squeeze you when you have to make a sale.

To me, the perfect customer is someone I can turn to and honestly say, 'Look, I really need to clear 10 per cent on this project. Here are my costs and here is where I expect to make my profit.'

What Do You Want the Customer to Do?

I'm not usually playing the role of buyer in business. Most of the time I'm selling (because I prefer asking for money to being asked for it). But inevitably I'm drawn into meetings with people who are clearly trying to sell me something.

Such was the case a few months ago when, as a favor to someone, I agreed to see a young man who, I was told, had an interesting concept. After 30 minutes of talk, I only had a vague idea of his concept – a 'foolproof' market research service – but I wasn't sure what he wanted from me. Was he selling me the service or seeking free advice or searching for start-up capital?

So I asked him, 'What do you want me to do next?'

'I want you to buy,' he said. 'I'd like you to become our first client, and I'd like you to tell others to become clients, too.'

A blunt answer for a blunt question. But I think it totally misses the point of what salespeople and customers really do. Getting the customer to buy, by definition, is the end-game of any sales strategy. Before you reach the end-game, however, there are any number of things an effective salesperson should want the customer to do. If anyone asked me, here are the first three things I would want my customers to do.

1 Don't waste my time.

There's nothing more cruel than a customer who strings you along. I'd rather deal with someone who negotiates every deal point down to the bare minimum. As wearisome as it may be, at least I know there's a sale at the end of all our jousting.

But you will always run across customers who can't admit they don't have the money or authority to buy from you or that they're simply not interested. It's often difficult to spot these people, in large part because of 'seller's denial'. After working so hard to track down a lead or get a foot in a door, salespeople don't want to admit to themselves that a prospect is a dead end. They think they'll break down the prospect's resistance with one more sales call. They convince themselves that they're building a relationship with each successive meeting. They want to stay in touch because it would tear them up to find out at some future date that the customer bought from someone else. (Believe me, I know that feeling.)

In most cases, hanging around is a fool's errand. Take a look at the best salespeople in your company. How many sales calls do they spend on a prospect before moving on? I suspect the answer is two or three. Now pose the same question to the struggling salespeople. I'd bet anything they make twice as many sales calls before they see the light. In other words, they waste twice as much time walking down cul de sacs.

It's not that the best salespeople are hit-and-run artists, jumping indiscriminately from prospect to prospect. On the contrary, top salespeople discriminate ruthlessly on the first or second sales call, by asking customers point blank, 'I know your time is valuable. Is this meeting wasting it?' Top salespeople are not afraid of the answer because they know it's the first thing they must get the customer to do. Struggling salespeople are too scared to ask.

2   Admit you have a problem.

Customers can't admit they have a problem because sometimes they don't know they do. It's not that customers are stupid. It may be that they are not as smart as you are in certain areas.

For example, I know very little about automobiles other than that I own and drive one. I know nothing about the mechanics of a car. I don't pay attention to gas mileage or annual maintenance cost, which are actually crucial factors in determining which model most people buy. My car could be costing three times more in annual repair costs than a comparable model, but because of my lack of expertise and general indifference to cars, I wouldn't know I had a problem.

A sharp salesperson would get me to admit I have a problem. The moment I walked into his dealership, he would ask me what I currently drive. (If he's really sharp he would have noted the car I came in.) If I'm driving a high-maintenance model, he would ask what I'm spending on repairs and how do I feel about that. Since the purchase of a car is often an 'emotional buy' – people are swayed by styling or power or blind loyalty to a brand rather than after-sale economics – pursuing the maintenance cost line might push an emotional hot button I didn't know I had. All things being equal, if the salesperson's line of cars are cheaper to maintain, he might make a sale. But he wouldn't stand a chance if he didn't first get me to do something – admit I had a problem.

It's the same in any business. Prospects who let you into their office want to hear how good you are. But more than anything else, they want to tell you how good they are too. If you hear them out, they'll give you openings to probe for problems. Probe shrewdly and they'll confess their weak spots. When people admit they have a problem, they immediately look for solutions, usually from the people to whom they admit it. Make sure that person is you.

3   Like me.

Customers have dozens of reasons not to buy from you. They don't need what you're selling. They know a competitor who is cheaper or better or quicker. They don't understand you. They understand but they don't believe you. These are serious, sometimes excusable hurdles. But there's no excuse for losing a sale because the customer doesn't like you.

I've always said that one of the watershed events in my career was the realization that I was losing out on a lot of opportunities because people didn't like me. I was representing Palmer, Nicklaus, and Player, the three biggest names in golf at the time. I thought the world would beat down my door to get to my clients. In fact, the world did. Selling Palmer, Nicklaus, and Player was a matter of answering the phone, quoting a price, and moving on to the next call.

In my mind, I was being hyper-efficient in a frantic seller's market. In other people's minds, I was abrupt and arrogant. And it had consequences. It puzzled me that many of the up-and-coming golfers on the tour deliberately avoided our company to sign with less experienced managers, until a friend pointed out the obvious. They didn't like me because I didn't take the time to get to know them or make them like me. Business picked up considerably the moment I changed my ways.

One of the great ironies in business is how many successful people acquire reputations for being difficult and uncompromising, yet when you meet them they are surprisingly disarming and affable. It's not because their reputation is undeserved or they have somehow been forced to suspend their true nature in your singular presence. They are like that with everyone. They can be tough if the situation demands it, but in the face of a potential customer, they know what they want the customer to do. They want you to like them. And they behave accordingly.

Getting the Reaction You Deserve

Some years ago the chairman emeritus of a company we were eager to work with offered to 'guide' me through the upper echelons of his old organization. I immediately accepted the offer. It's not every day you get an expert tour of the inner workings of a major customer.

My first lesson was some tutoring about the current CEO and the five executives who made up the Office of the President. The chairman emeritus had personally hired everyone in the group, so his thumbnail sketches of each executive were more insightful than the data supplied in the official biographies and press releases.

Of the CEO, he said, 'Don't be put off if he seems noncommital at first. He reacts slowly to everything.'

'The marketing chief,' he said, 'is an enthusiast. He responds positively to every idea. But don't be surprised if he changes his mind the next day.'

Of the chief financial officer, he said, 'He reacts negatively to anything. That's his job.'

Even a slow study could pick up the retired chairman's theme: Anyone can see how a person reacts to his or her sales pitch. But you need some historical perspective to understand what those reactions really mean.

In hindsight, the chairman's analysis of reaction styles was probably the most valuable advice he could give me. It gave me an edge that I'd never considered before. It eliminated any false impressions I had about our prospects at the company. It warned me not to take anything at face value. I shouldn't get my hopes up because of one executive's enthusiasm. Likewise, I shouldn't be discouraged by another executive's initial negative reaction. Plugging away would probably turn that person around.

Since that episode I've always tried to learn something about how people react to information or questions – and put it to use both as a manager and salesperson. Here are four common ways people react.

1 Slow reactors.

I admire slow reactors (and wish I were more like them). No matter how much you value quickness and decisiveness, you will rarely get into trouble or lose out on an opportunity because you react slowly.

Slow reactors play their cards close to the vest. In a

negotiation, they keep the other side slightly off balance because they never reveal what they're really thinking. In a sales situation, they can't be hurried into making a deal they don't like. They can walk away and wait for a better offer. In a world where people are constantly being rushed into decisions they later regret, I believe this tortoise-like discipline is incredibly valuable.

I also like managing slow reactors – because I know they will keep cool in crises and that their opinions are based on careful reflection rather than panic or a need to demonstrate a speedy response. In fact, I try to promote slower reactions in our company. When I make a suggestion or pose a question to subordinates, I often preface it by telling them, 'You don't need to answer this right now. Get back to me in a couple of days.' I want them to know it's alright to slow down, that the quick answer is useless if it isn't also the right answer.

2   Negative reactors.

Negative reactors automatically hate any suggestion. They are constitutionally incapable of saying, 'I like that,' or 'That's a great idea.' Actually, they're easy to deal with if you can tune in to the finely calibrated meanings of their various 'No's'.

We used to have an executive who was a classic negative reactor. I knew that about him, so I would always discount his first or second reactions to my suggestions. If I asked him if he would be interested in representing a new client, I knew that his immediate 'No' probably meant yes, 'Absolutely not!' meant maybe, and 'I will quit before I work with that jerk!' was a solid no. Only if I heard the last remark would I give up my efforts to get him to do my bidding.

To managers, negative reactors are extremely useful as messengers. They seem to enjoy telling people no. I know because I've been on the receiving end of these scenarios. There have been times when I knew a decision-maker didn't want to be the one to turn down one of our proposals, so he would turn over the decision to one of his associates – invariably the in-house negative reactor. He may tell me, 'I'll go along with this if Joe Smith likes it,' but both of us know the answer.

3   Nuclear reactors.

Nuclear reactors are people who overreact to everything. To them, your price isn't merely high, it's 'outrageous'. Your idea isn't just weak; it's the 'dumbest idea I've ever heard'. Your negotiating position isn't just a dealbreaker; it's the 'reason we'll never do business with you again'. If a response can be taken to the extreme, they'll take it. And they'll do it loudly, impulsively, intemperately, and sometimes irrationally.

There are only two times when this type of reaction is useful: when you want to intimidate someone and when someone is trying to intimidate you.

4   Calculated reactors.

There are some extraordinary people who have total control over their reactions. Depending on the news they're hearing and the kind of message they want to send back, they can assume a posture of inscrutability, volcanic rage, affability, enthusiasm, or whatever else is called for. This is acting, not reacting.

This can be a valuable talent. I know there are times when I've wished that I had reacted more slowly to a bulletin, when I've blurted something out and immediately wished that I could take it back. A greater degree of calculation in my reactions would make me a better salesman, negotiator and manager.

Of course, there's a downside to this. Once recognized, calculated reactors can never be trusted. They always have a hidden agenda. Regardless of their response to a situation, they always leave other people wondering what that agenda may be.

How to Rate a Meeting (or My Favorite Hidden Agendas)

An associate and I made a sales call on an apparel company a few months ago. The meeting had taken months to set up, but it gave us a chance to spend an hour with the company's three top officers. As we left the building, my associate turned to me and said, 'Well, that was a complete waste of time.'

'What do you mean?' I said. 'I thought it was a great meeting.'

'Of course you would, Mark,' he said. 'All your meetings are great. I've never heard you say you've had a bad meeting.'

Beneath the gentle sarcasm in that remark, my associate had a point. There's a part of me that refuses to admit my sales calls are totally pointless.

Some of this is a mental game. Selling is a tough, frustrating business that can chip away at your enthusiasm and wear down your spirit. Looking at your sales calls through rose-tinted glasses is one way to stay motivated.

But it's not the only way. What my associate didn't appreciate was that I have a very forgiving grading system for my sales calls. My expectations are usually modest. My criteria for a 'great' meeting have little to do with making a sale or, for that matter, even pitching a specific concept. Sometimes the only item on my agenda is finding out whether I like the customer or he likes me.

My associate was discouraged by three facts that came out in our meeting: the company had a limited advertising budget; they had never spent marketing dollars on athletes or sporting events; and none of the three officers was particularly passionate about sports. No money. No precedents. No interest. Those are three big obstacles if you're selling any marketing concept. I can see why, to him, the glass was half empty.

I saw a different picture. I saw a senior management that was very smart and a company that was growing rapidly. If they didn't have the budget now, they might have it in 12 months. If they didn't like sports, they might be open to an idea in, say, classical music. In that sense it was a great meeting. Here was a company worth revisiting in a few months. The glass, in fact, was half full – and might soon be fuller.

Here is a checklist of some of my favorite sales call agendas. My goals, you'll see, are quite simple. But that usually means I'm more likely to achieve them.

1 Do you like the customer?

This is the most important piece of information you can pick up from a meeting. If you like the prospect, you're more likely to keep calling on him or her. If you continue calling, over time you are more likely to do business together – even though at the outset there is no compelling economic or strategic reason for you to do so. The obvious corrolary here is: Does the customer like you? That's important data too.

For 15 years now, whenever I am in Tokyo, I've made a point of having breakfast with the Japanese chief of a major office equipment manufacturer. We meet because we like each other. I regard him as a friend.

In all that time we never did business together (even though his company has worked with athletes from one of our competitors). Not long ago he asked me if we had any ideas to help his company celebrate its 75th anniversary. I suggested a gala concert tour with our client Itzhak Perlman – and he bought the concept on the spot.

You could say it took me 15 years to make that sale. But in my mind, I closed the deal 15 years before – at our first meeting when I realized that this gentleman was someone I liked, someone who could be a friend, someone I enjoyed staying in touch with.

In a sales career, you'll meet a lot of customers with whom you don't have much in common. So don't ignore those rare occasions when you meet someone who is totally sympatico with you. A meeting in which you find a friend is a great meeting.

2 Do they like sports?

If I can determine that the customer likes sports (and which sports in particular) at a meeting, then I know I'm not wasting my time. A customer who is passionate about sports will usually find a way to use sports in his marketing mix.

3 Why are they doing business with the competition?

I like to call on customers who are buying sports concepts from our competitors but not from us – so I can ask them why. I may not change their mind at the meeting. But their explanation will tell me what our company is doing wrong. And that I can change.

4 What do they think our company does?

A lot of potential customers have misconceptions about our company. They think we're too big (or not big enough). They think we only do 'big' deals and that they can't afford us. They don't know the extent of our operations overseas. They think we're only involved in golf or tennis.

Sometimes my only agenda in a meeting is to disabuse the customer of these misconceptions. I may not get him excited about anything in particular that day, but if I can deliver the message that we can create inexpensive concepts and not only in sports, I've got him thinking about us in a new light.

5 Do they have a budget?

Before you can convince the customer to spend money on you, you have to determine if he has any money to spend. If he doesn't have the budget now, will he have it in the near future? The answer to that question tells me if and when I need to schedule a second meeting.

6 Is there an 'emotional' buyer in the building?

I'm always looking for the real decision-maker in a meeting. But over the years, I've learned that sports is not always a rational 'by the numbers' buy. Sometimes it's an emotional buy. (It's hard to explain but it's no different from a car buyer who has an emotional need to buy a Corvette or a Ferrari. No other nameplate will do.) And so, I often go into a meeting looking for a decision-maker who has an emotional need to be involved with, say, Wimbledon or the British Open. If I find him, I can save myself months, maybe years of selling. We can agree on terms in minutes – and sidestep all the lawyers and technocrats that make a sale so time-consuming. A meeting that identifies an emotional buyer may be the best meeting of all.

It Doesn't Take Much to Keep the Customer Happy

One of the great business myths is that you have to go all out every day to keep your customers and clients happy. While giving your best at all times is admirable, advisable, and preferable, it's not necessarily true.

The real picture is that customers and clients are very

forgiving. Once they commit to being your customer or client, you have to mess up in a major way and mess up often before they'll admit they were wrong to hire you.

I know what I'm talking about. As a fairly demanding customer myself, I still shake my head in amazement at how much incompetence I'll tolerate from merchants and suppliers before I take my business elsewhere. I'm not bragging and I'm certainly not endorsing negligence as a customer-retention strategy. I'm just making the observation that it doesn't take much to keep most customers on board.

Yet a lot of people still manage to fall short of this bare minimum and watch their prized customers and clients walk out the door.

When you boil it all down, your customers and clients use three criteria to measure you:
- Communication
- Service
- Added value

How well you handle these three items is a reliable indicator of how long you'll keep your clients. Here is a checklist to see how you're doing:

1 Communication

We all have enough sense to communicate well before the sale. That's when we're alert, when we're willing to explain everything to the client, when we return the client's calls immediately, when we cater to the client's every whim.

But it's even more important to communicate after the

sale. That's when a lot of us fall short. With the client safely in hand, we start taking him for granted.

Are you accessible? Do you hear as well as listen? Do you accept, as a given, that the client's priorities are different from, and more important than, your priorities?

Most important, do you work overtime at explaining why? Clients expect you to explain the who, what, when, where, and how much of any transaction. And most of us are pretty good at that. But whenever there is a communication breakdown, it's almost always because someone forgot to explain why. That's the missing ingredient that customers really want.

A rudimentary example: Let's say I take my car in for a $100 tune-up. I pick it up later that day, where I'm handed a $600 repair bill. The mechanic goes through the bill with me. 'That's $20 for an oil change, $30 for new spark plugs, $50 for labour . . . and $420 for new brakes.' In other words, he's communicating the what and how much. But given the inherent paranoia that all of us feel in an auto repair shop (cars are a mystery and we're going to get fleeced), that mechanic better have a brilliant explanation for that surprise $420 charge for new brakes. He's going to have to do better than saying, 'They were worn out.' If he tells me why – by showing me the old brakes, pointing out the damage, citing that they tend to wear out after so many miles, etc. – I might not find the bill so hard to swallow. And if he volunteers that why before I have to ask for it, I'll be even more impressed. I'll drive out of the shop grateful to him. He has a customer for life.

2 Service

At this late date, I don't think any more ink needs to be spilled over the concept of service. It has been the defining issue on the international business scene for the past decade. If the customer is faced with two equivalent products, the reason he usually chooses one over the other is service. The promise of excellent service is how you win new customers and clients.

What many of us forget, however, is that the continued delivery of that service is how you keep clients. It's good business. In the long run, it costs a lot less to hold onto existing clients than to find new ones.

My friend, Ben Bidwell, the former chairman of Chrysler Motors, cited the example of how the American auto industry forgot this simple concept.

'My industry chased new business every day of the year,' he told me. 'It was where we invested all of our money – in advertising, rebates, product development. While we were doing that, we were telling the customers that we already had "Sorry, your warranty doesn't cover that," or "Sorry, we don't have a fix for that."

'We got what we deserved. We once calculated that it cost Chrysler nearly $10,000 per person to bring a new customer into the showroom and sell him a car. And we were doing this while we were losing old customers who would have stayed with us with a $100 bill here and there. It was crazy.'

If you don't appreciate the importance of service by now, just look at your current client list. Think how much easier it is to service them properly than to replace them with new clients.

3 Added value

This is the toughest criterion to measure and deliver – because what is added value in your mind (i.e., extraordinary service that is way beyond the call of duty) may be standard procedure in one client's mind and totally unnecessary in another's.

We face this in our client business all the time.

Some clients come to us simply to increase their income. Measuring added value is a numbers game with them: How much did they earn before they came to us and how much are they earning with us? They don't care about all the extraordinary service we provide. It has no value to them.

Other clients come to us precisely for that service. A classical music superstar asks us to represent him not because he wants us to book more concert dates for him. He usually has more offers than he can handle. What he's looking for is the personal touch, someone who's not only interested in shaping his career but who will take his call any hour of the day to handle the most niggling detail. To this sort of client, added value is measured by how unpleasant his life would be without us.

The thing to remember about added value is that it varies with every client. Before you can add value to a client relationship, you have to know what the client actually values.

When I mentioned these three categories to a friend not long ago, he reminded me that you don't have to do all three to hold on to a client.

'If you're good at two out of three,' he said, 'your clients will stay with you and most of them will be happy. You can probably get away with being good at one of the three.'

When I asked him which of the three categories he values most, he unequivocally answered, 'Communication'. Then he told me about his financial advisor.

'In terms of added value,' he said, 'my advisor has given me virtually nothing. In some instances, his advice has cost me money. Going strictly by the numbers, I could do as well without him. I don't need him to park my money in a savings account. So if you measure added value by what he has brought to the party, he comes up a zero.

'But he's terrific when it comes to service and communication. I get all my statements on time. They're accurate. If I have an investment question, he gets back to me with a well-researched answer. It's hard to fault him on service. That's why I stay with him. How do I know I'll do better with someone else?

'But what really clinches it is that he has a well-reasoned explanation for every investment decision. His moves don't always pan out. But, hey, nobody's perfect. As long as he's telling me why he does what he does, I can live with his results. Maybe that's foolish. But that's the big reason I stay.'

As I say, it doesn't take much to keep clients happy. Sometimes the bare minimum will do.

The Harder You Try, the Harder They Try

There comes a point in every protracted sale where the salesperson must make a choice. He has done everything in his power to get the customer to commit – meetings, proposals, product demonstrations, follow-up calls, etc. But the customer remains undecided.

Should the salesperson keep plugging away at the

customer, risking more of his time and energy on what may be a hopeless cause? Or should he cut his losses and move on to something else?

With rare exceptions, I would always choose to keep plugging away – because in the long run people cannot resist someone who tries so hard to please them. It's only human nature. People are mimics. The more you try, the more they have to respond in kind.

I see this sort of mimicking all the time on the tennis court – when one player starts hitting the ball with a lot of pace and the other player instinctively returns the shot with equal pace (even when he knows it's bad for his game).

I also see it constantly in sales situations.

A few years ago we were very interested in representing the literary and broadcast interests of a retired public figure. But we were having a tough time convincing him he needed an agent. No matter how eloquently we outlined all the wonderful things we could do for him around the globe, he still resisted us.

This unrequited courtship went on for months until one day he mentioned to me that he was planning a trip to Japan. I immediately seized upon this information – and put our Tokyo office at his disposal. No longer would we be telling him how good we are. This was a chance to show him.

I sensed that as our Tokyo office got involved in booking his flights and hotels, introducing him to Japanese business people, and setting up interviews with local media, he could no longer straddle the fence about working with us. He would be in constant communication with our people. The harder we worked, the less he could resist us. Although there was no money involved and we were basically doing him a favor, during his stay in Japan he would be our de facto client.

After that, if we did our job well, signing him up as a real client would be a formality. Which is exactly what happened.

Worry About the Payoff Later

I've always thought that one of the biggest mistakes salespeople make, particularly when they are selling a service, is refusing to work with a prospect until they have an agreement or some money changes hands. I can understand why people adopt this attitude. We all want to get paid for our time and talent, and there's a natural suspicion that someone will take advantage of us.

In my experience, you are always better off getting entangled with a potential customer – and worrying about the payoff later.

I realized this quite by accident in my first year in business – when we began doing what we called checkbook reconciliations for our golf clients. It seemed to me that a client like Arnold Palmer should have an idea where his money was going. So we created a report listing every incoming and outgoing check, and the beginning and closing balance for the month. This sort of reporting is common now, but it wasn't back in 1961. I should also note that we didn't get paid for doing this. It was simply the smart thing to do.

But getting involved with someone else's checkbook forced us to live up to a whole new set of expectations. We had to have answers when the client asked, 'Why did I spend this money?' or 'Could you track down this bill?' It gave us the opportunity to demonstrate how good we were at chasing down a bill, which in turn led to more and more services that the client required of us. The harder we worked to please the clients, the more they had to include us in their affairs. Our extra effort was a form of salesmanship.

The side benefit was not something I could have predicted. The expertise we were forced to develop in financial management, taxes, and insurance not only cemented our relationship with clients but helped the company grow.

When to Fire Your Customers

A salesperson's agenda is simple: Move product. Build up volume. Sell to whoever is willing to buy.

In managing salespeople, you don't usually want them to complicate this process by being selective about who they sell to – and, in general, you don't encourage them to let customers or clients walk out the door. But perhaps you should. Some clients and customers, no matter how willing they are to buy your product or service, simply are not worth it.

The most obvious customer to avoid is the one who doesn't pay on time. No matter how painful it is to turn away business, a slow-paying customer makes you look bad, frustrates your bankers, and destroys your cash flow and credibility. A slow-paying customer also distracts you from selling and forces you into the collection business.

Almost as dangerous as the customer who doesn't pay is the customer who pays too much.

A few years ago we received an offer from a foreign

entertainment group that wanted the services of two superstar clients for a series of instructional videos. The amount of money this group was offering – backed up by letters of credit – was mind-boggling. In fact, the offer was so high, so out of line with industry standards, that we knew there was no way they could recoup their investment.

So we turned them down.

For one thing, we didn't respect their judgment. If they were so misguided at pricing our clients' contributions, they would probably be incompetent at producing and marketing the videos as well.

More importantly, we knew that long after the deal was done, what people in our business would remember was not the quality of the videos or our clients' contributions but that the project lost money. They'd forget that a group of business people made a foolish offer. What would linger most vividly in their minds was that our clients were involved in a loser.

Then there are the customers or clients who not only do nothing to enhance your reputation but can actually damage it. Years ago we sold the Ford Motor Co. on the concept of using one of our top tennis clients to play an exhibition in Detroit. This was the third year that Ford had sponsored the event and it was extremely important to them. At the last minute, our client pulled out, claiming he was sick in Brazil. Two days later the Ford people read in the newspaper that he was playing in Hong Kong. So, to keep the relationship with Ford, we fired the client.

In a sense, jettisoning customers and clients who don't bring in money or who threaten your reputation isn't that tough a call. The trickier calls involve the marginal clients who are slightly profitable and don't put too much strain on your time and resources. How do you decide which marginal clients to keep and which to fire?

This happened to us in London two decades back when we started representing Jean Shrimpton, the top model in the world at the time. Shrimpton had retired from day-to-day modeling and asked us to bring her endorsement deals. We did such a good job that Shrimpton persuaded her fellow superstar Verushka to sign with us. Then we started working for a third model named Maudie James. The only problem was that Maudie James wasn't retired and interested only in endorsements. She wanted to work every day. She needed a booking agent, not a representative. At the time, the nearest thing we had to a booking agent in our London office was the switchboard operator who fielded calls for Maudie James and said, 'I'll get back to you'. No one else wanted to do the job.

These three models paid us $50,000 a year in commissions. Yet all our people were advising me to fire Shrimpton, Verushka, and James and get out of the business.

I responded, 'Well, if we fire the models, who are we going to fire from the staff? If we don't do that to reduce our expenses, all we've done is say goodbye to $50,000 from our bottom line.'

Fortunately, none of our people had a good answer for that. And we're still in the modeling business, only bigger and better.

Is the Customer Entitled to All My Time?

One of our senior financial executives once expressed some concern about all the time demands put on him by some of his clients. He mentioned one incident where he was dining with his wife at a Cleveland club. During the course of a pleasant meal, one of his financial clients spotted him and joined him at the table to ask him some serious questions about his investment portfolio.

Our executive was a little peeved at the intrusion and puzzled about how to react. 'Where do you draw the line?' he asked me. 'Is a client entitled to all my time?'

I don't think he was really complaining – because he instinctively did the right thing: he handled the situation on the spot. He allayed an obviously concerned client's doubts at the table.

He answered his own question, 'Is the client entitled to all my time?' with an unequivocal 'Yes' because he understood some fundamental rules about dealing with clients or customers, such as:

1 'Great service' is defined by the client.

You can be doing the best job in the world for your client, but if there's something missing, if the client is unhappy, then all your opinions about your performance are worthless. Great service is a matter of perception. Great service is what the client thinks it is.

Ironically, most clients or customers make it fairly easy for you to provide great service. They're not abusive or overdemanding. They don't expect you to be on 24-hour call or to jump through hoops. But they do expect you to come through in a 'crisis'.

The typical crisis in most service businesses – whether you're selling electrical appliances, running a hotel, delivering overnight mail, or servicing office equipment – is *a customer with a complaint*.

In fact, in my experience as both a provider and consumer of services, complaints are *the defining moments* in most buyer-seller relationships. How you handle a complaint – whether you solve it on the spot or make the customer scratch and claw for satisfaction – usually spells the difference between great service and its absence. At least it does in the customer's mind, which after all is the only opinion that matters.

2   Divide your time, not your attention.

A British publisher I know has enormous admiration for a rival publisher, particularly his ability to attract and publish major female authors. This rival is not attractive in any conventional sense. He's homely looking and fairly well along in years. Yet he appears to be irresistible to women.

My publishing friend asked one of his female authors what was his secret.

'There's no secret,' said the lady. 'Unlike most people, he gives you his complete and undivided attention. You can be in a room swirling with famous and beautiful faces, but he will never take his eyes off you. For those moments you spend in each other's company, you are the only person in the world who matters. That's very intoxicating.'

I think that principle applies in any situation. If clients and customers get your undivided attention when you are with them, it won't matter how you divide your time elsewhere.

3   Clients want a long-term relationship, too.

Nearly everything we do in our organization is geared to fostering long-term relationships – because that's what propels you during the boom years and sustains you during the lean ones.

If long-term relationships are important to us as the seller, it follows then that they are equally important to the customer. Yet this is something many people in sales organizations don't fully appreciate.

To them, a win-win situation is one where they provide a product or service and the customer provides money. That's not a relationship, it's a transaction. They forget that the customer expects his patronage to add up to something greater than the sum of his spending.

I know this is true, because of how I feel when I am the customer. If I patronize the corner grocery store once a week, at some point I'd expect the proprietor to acknowledge me or remember my name. If I frequent a particular restaurant, I'd expect to be recognized and perhaps seated at my favorite table. That's one of the psychological benefits of being a loyal customer.

The same thing happens on a corporate level. At some point, you have to show the customer that he is part of a relationship, not a series of transactions.

This can manifest itself in many ways, from giving the customer your home phone number (so he can call you anytime) to bombarding him with information or ideas (so he knows you're thinking about him) to giving him greater access to your company's resources.

For example, as I write this, I'm sure there are at least a dozen people within our organization who are doing something for a client for which we are not getting paid –

anything from securing tickets to a sold-out sporting event to reserving a rental car to answering a legal question to researching a marketing idea. While there's a tiny part of me that might wish we got paid for this effort, I derive great comfort from knowing that in the long-term we will.

4 One unhappy customer can wipe out 100 happy ones.

Fear is probably the biggest force behind any extraordinary effort for a client. Fear of disappointing the client. Fear of losing the client. Fear that the client will tell someone else.

Keep that in mind the next time you waver between going the extra mile for your client and trying to slide by. If you don't feel fear, you're probably in the wrong business (or soon will be out of business). The truth is, one unhappy customer can wipe out the positive comments of 100 satisfied ones.

Getting Customer Entertainment Right

A friend once asked me what I considered the most effective venue for entertaining potential customers. Is it an expensive dinner? Tickets to a Broadway or West End show? A round of golf? Chartering a deep-sea fishing boat?

Any one of these venues can provide a glorious experience – or end up in disaster. The fact is, entertaining customers properly (so they like you, so you learn something about them, and so they might consider buying from you in the future) is not so much a function of venue but rather of three often overlooked factors. (1) The experience has to be unique. (2) It must be executed well. (3) It should somehow enhance your relationship.

1   Uniqueness.

Venue is one of the more misunderstood aspects of entertaining, particularly when salespeople think that winning a customer over is simply a matter of how much money they spend on him. I don't buy that. If it were true, the best salespeople would only go to the most expensive restaurants. They would only buy front-row seats at the ballpark. And you could identify your most productive salespeople simply by how much they spent on T&E.

Entertaining takes a little more thought than pulling out a credit card or emptying your wallet.

In my experience, anywhere can be the ideal place to take your customers as long as it is unique. My rule is take them somewhere they couldn't go without me.

For example, taking a customer to a Broadway show is a nice gesture. If we have dinner, it can also be expensive. But it's not really unique. Anyone can buy a ticket. And it really doesn't take advantage of our company's involvement in sports.

If I take the customer to a sold-out football game, probably anyone with a little effort can buy a seat.

If I take him to the Super Bowl, possibly anyone with a few thousand dollars can get a seat.

If I take him to Wimbledon and invite him into a tent to meet some of the tennis players, he probably couldn't do that without me.

If I take him to play golf with Arnold Palmer, I'm certain he couldn't do that without me.

Thus, in my scheme of things, on a scale of 1 to 10 with 10 being the most unique, the Broadway show is a 1. Golf with Arnold is a 10.

2   Execution.

No matter how unique the experience, it's even more important to execute it well. One of our executives once jumped through hoops to obtain last-minute tickets to the Yale-Harvard football game for a major customer. Unfortunately, the seats were behind a post. This wasn't a major disaster. The customer appreciated our effort. But our less-than-stellar execution negated whatever benefits we derived from doing someone a favor.

Another time, one of our executives gave up his U.S. Open tennis tickets because the chairman of a French company that we had dealt with for many years was eager to see one of his countrymen play that evening. We warned this courtly gentleman that the seats were closer to the sky than to the court. He said it didn't matter. Of course, by the time he got to his seat near the top of the stadium, it did matter. He was offended at being so far away from the action. One of his assistants later told us that we would have been better off saying we couldn't help him. That's the danger of faulty execution. The chairman forgets that someone in our office secured him tickets at the last minute. He only remembers that they were lousy.

The real secret to great execution is to throw in a surprise or extra ingredient. When Lufthansa invites customers to the Monaco Grand Prix, they don't just drop off the guests at a hotel and leave them on their own for the weekend. They go the extra mile to make it special. They hire our client Jackie Stewart as their host. Jackie takes the guests through the pits where the cars are being prepared. He introduces the guests to the drivers. He teaches them how to watch a race. He ushers them onto a minibus and drives the course, explaining 'At this point, you're going 98 mph and you have to downshift for that hairpin turn. . . .' With that kind of execution, I don't think the guests would be disappointed even if race day was disastrous.

3   Enhancement.

The third element in customer entertainment is how the effort enhances the relationship. The key here is to create a situation where you can actually talk to the person.

You can't do that in a theater. Even if you have great seats at a must-see show (i.e., you've scored a 10 for both uniqueness and execution), the truth is you and the customer are still sitting in a dark theater next to each other in silence watching. Other than your dramatic tastes, what have you learned about the customer and what has he learned about you?

Another common practice I don't understand: passing along tickets to an event but not attending yourself. This is getting customer entertainment half right (and half wrong). You've created a debt, the feeling of 'I owe you one,' but what have you done to enhance the relationship?

Oddly enough, if you give more thought to how you enhance the relationship, you don't have to try so hard on making it unique or even executing it well.

For example, we once created a customer entertainment function for a weekly magazine. The magazine invited the CEOs of its major advertisers to play golf for three days in Scotland.

How unique is that? Anyone can play golf in Scotland. In fact, most of the CEOs had done so many times. So, on a scale of 1 to 10, perhaps that's a 2 for uniqueness.

How well was it executed? Since the executives were playing with Scottish golf pros in a very elegant setting, the execution rates an 8.

But the magazine's people scored a solid 10 in terms of improving their relationship with their advertisers. The big reason, I think, is because they gave themselves three days – on the fairways and at breakfast, lunch, and dinner – to talk to and listen to their prime customers. The attractive setting and leisurely ambiance obviously didn't hurt. But months from now, when everyone is doing business together, what will linger in the attendees' minds are not the scores they posted on some Scottish golf course but the insights and friendships they formed there.

That's the desired effect, and easily achieved, when you get customer entertainment right.

How to Develop Repeat Customers

Success in business is a lot like being a number-one ranked athlete. Getting to the top is tough enough, but staying there is even harder.

Nowhere is this more evident than in selling – where you're only as good as your most recent closing. The most successful people, however, have a secret: the 80/20 rule.

They realize that in most companies 80 per cent of your

business comes from 20 per cent of your customers. And so they make it easy on themselves. They knock on old doors. They don't sell to strangers. They sell to their existing customers, because someone who has bought from you once is more likely to buy from you again.

How you instill the desire to buy in a person who has bought from you once but has no apparent reason to buy from you again is perhaps the greatest selling skill. Here are six ways to convert first-time buyers into regulars:

1   Sell the market, then the product.

In the sports marketing business, our company is regarded as a pioneer and the market leader. So part of our sales effort has always been educating customers about sports. Before we try to sell them our brand of sports marketing, we have to get them excited about sports in general. We're willing to take our chances on whether they eventually do business with us. Experience has taught us that if a company becomes dedicated to sports, we'll pick up a little or a lot of their business.

Customers come back to us because of the market we're in, not because of our market share.

2   Service first, selling second.

The moment a customer buys into one of our projects, we're faced with a dilemma: Do we service the sale? Or while he has his checkbook out, do we try to sell him something else?

The tendency in our company is to devote all our efforts

to servicing that sale and maximizing the benefits for the customer and ourselves. It's a lot easier to go back to a customer with a certified success behind you than without one.

3   Share the wealth with your peers.

In our organization we put a premium on inter-divisional cooperation. That's often the key to generating repeat business. A customer who is already doing business with our golf division may not have the budget or the need for more golf projects. But this same customer may be intrigued by a concept from our tennis or winter sports division. It's my job as a manager to encourage colleagues to share the wealth with their peers.

Unfortunately, this is not as easy as it sounds. There's a part of all of us that gets possessive with a customer or client. We don't want someone to dilute our relationship, or become a better friend of that customer, or siphon funds from our profit center, or take the credit for our spade-work. A compensation system that recognizes and rewards cooperation – that shares the wealth with those who share, if you will – will usually cure this problem.

4   Use the calendar.

In the right hands, a calendar is a sales tool.

Nearly every customer has some dates during the calendar year when he is more willing or able to buy and, consequently, most vulnerable to a sales effort. Florists, for example, know that people buy flowers around certain

holidays. So they remind their customers (with advertise-
ments, flyers, and letters) and get their repeat business
several times a year – each year.

A similar pattern exists in corporate sales. Fiscal years
vary among corporations. But nearly every company is
more willing to buy at the beginning of the fiscal year,
when the coffers are full, then at the end.

5   Think small to get big.

When it comes to generating repeat business, there are
several compelling reasons to think small. Small sales are
easier to close, easier to service, and far less risky to your
reputation. Mess up a small deal and the customer may
forgive you. Mess up a big deal and the customer may not
be around to buy again.

I find it's helpful to think of customers as revenue
streams. If you start with a trickle, the flood will come later.

For example, I have a reputation for asking big numbers. But some of my best sales have been very small. I
once called on a company about an expensive client-
entertainment concept. Minutes into our discussion, it was
apparent that their plans weren't nearly as grandiose in
scope as I had imagined. So I shrunk the proposal,
suggesting that they take four people to a prize fight and
let us arrange the evening for them. They agreed. To me
that's a success. It gives us a foot in the door at their
company, gets them used to seeing our face, and starts
them thinking of us as a business resource. If we do our job
well, we may never have to call on them again. They will
call us.

6   Don't sell reliability short.

No matter how well you master the five points above, when all is said and done there's no magic to winning repeat customers. The successful executives in our organization are the people who deliver what they say they will deliver when they say they're going to deliver it at a cost that they originally quoted. That's a rare combination. Customers will rush to do business over and over again with people like that.

Why Is Everyone Telling You No?

In a motivational talk to his buyers, Stanley Marcus, the legendary merchant and founder of the Neiman-Marcus retail chain, once told this macabre story about a vendor named Mr Walker who had been trying to sell his product line to a buyer at Bloomingdales department store named Mr Friedland. Mr Walker had been calling on Mr Friedland for 30 years with no success.

One morning Walker showed up at Bloomingdales and asked to see Mr Friedland.

With sadness in her voice, the receptionist informed him, I'm sorry, Mr Walker, but Mr Friedland passed away last week.'

Walker picked up his sample case and took a seat on the reception area sofa. After five minutes he approached the receptionist again and asked to see Mr Friedland.

'I'm sorry,' she said, 'but Mr Friedland is dead.'

Again Walker returned to the sofa. Again, five minutes passed and he asked to see Mr Friedland.

'Mr Friedland is dead,' said the receptionist.

This continued every five minutes for another hour. Finally, the receptionist asked Walker in exasperation, 'What's the matter with you? Don't you understand that Mr Friedland is dead?'

'Sure, I understand,' said Walker. 'I just love hearing you say it.'

Marcus's point to his buyers was that they ought to be nice to their vendors.

But he also could have pointed out how some salespeople, like Mr Walker, never recognize that some of the people they're calling on, no matter how they lead them on, will never buy from them.

There are many reasons why people say no, not all of them malicious:

• They may not have the guts to make a decision.
• They may not have the budget.
• They may not have the authority.
• They may not have the brains.
• Your proposal may be bad.

Whatever the reason, you have two courses of action when you run into these paragons of negativity. Avoid them, or get them to tell you what you're doing wrong.

1   Avoid them.

This is basically what we've been doing with a mid-level executive at a major American corporation. Over the years, he's been very polite and receptive to our ideas. He's always encouraging us to send our proposals his way.

But not once has he said yes to us. It's taken us years to

figure out that he is, in fact, his company's designated 'Doctor No'.

He is not really a decision-maker. He is a corporate gatekeeper, adept at ushering people into his quarters, making them feel good about him and his company, and then painlessly showing them the door. We've given up trying to fathom why he cannot make a commitment.

Our strategy now is to avoid him. We make sure our proposals never reach his desk. As a result, we are now doing a lot of business with his more decisive colleagues.

2 Let them tell you what you're doing wrong.

I learned this years ago from my friend, Ben Bidwell, when he was general manager of the Lincoln-Mercury division of Ford Motor Co.

Ben is a very decisive executive, not afraid of big numbers and making bold commitments. But you couldn't convince me of that over a period of several years when we were pummeling Lincoln-Mercury with proposal after proposal and always getting the same 'No'.

One day, either out of kindness or frustration, Ben called me up in Cleveland and said, 'Mark, if you would bring a couple of your people up here to our office and let us explain what it takes to get us to say yes, it would save both of us a lot of time in the future.'

This was an offer we couldn't refuse.

I took two of our executives up to Dearborn, Michigan, where over the course of several hours we were indoctrinated into what Ford was looking for, how we should present it, and to whom we should be sending it.

As a result of that meeting, Ford committed to sponsoring the World Invitational Tennis Classic. More important, I learned that if you're not sure what the buyer wants, let him tell you. It's much easier to sell a customer what he wants to buy than to convince him to buy what you are selling.

Don't Be Dazzled by Blue-Chip Customers

For years I have admonished our salespeople to assume almost nothing from the title of the person they were calling on. I tell them how I had always dreamt about getting a meeting with the head of General Motors International. I figured, 'GM is a huge company with huge spending habits in sports. If I could just get my foot in the door of the international division, my life would be made.'

I eventually got the meeting. As I ascended in the elevator in Manhattan's General Motors Building my heart was pounding.

Yet five minutes into the meeting I realized that there was virtually nothing the head of GM International could do for me. He had very little authority and, in effect, was a traffic cop for information between GM's numerous autonomous companies. Any fantasies I had about selling wholesale to GM ended in the international chief's office that day. I was undone by an impressive title.

Conversely, I once flew to Japan to discuss sponsorship of the woman's pro tennis tour with Toyota. The meeting took place in a bare office with just two chairs and a table. I found myself presenting to a welcoming committee of one, a young man whose business card told me he was an 'assistant manager' in the PR department. As I began explaining how the sponsorship worked – this much for this, another half-million dollars for the bonus pool – the assistant manager nodded his head in agreement. I must admit I felt a little foolish (and frankly, insulted) by the reception. I was offering a multi-year multi-million-dollar program. I was sure the assistant manager didn't have a clue about what I was describing and that he was just being polite to someone who had traveled a long distance. I also thought the scope of the project required a hearing from a slightly more senior manager. I left Japan dejected. A few weeks later Toyota informed us that they would buy the entire program.

These two contrasting incidents taught me never to put too much faith in job titles.

Over the years I've also learned that it's a mistake to put too much faith in the size and reputation of the companies you're calling on – whether that means you're over-impressed by a blue chip company or underwhelmed by a small startup operation.

We once determined that close to 4500 U.S. companies used sports and special events sponsorships as part of their marketing mix, spending more than $4.3 billion a year. That's a big playground for IMG. If we could capture a 25 per cent share of that market, we would be registering $1 billion in sales in the U.S. alone.

Looking at the 20 biggest customers, we found the usual suspects. Philip Morris led the pack, spending $110 million annually on sports sponsorships for brands such as Marlboro cigarettes and Miller beer. Anheuser-Busch, brewer of Budweiser and other beer brands, was next at $90 million, followed in descending order by Coca-Cola,

Kodak, General Motors, IBM, RJR Nabisco, Chrysler, Pepsico, AT&T, Dupont, McDonald's, and Quaker Oats. These are all giant companies with big appetites for sport. Together, the top 20 companies accounted for 17 per cent of all sponsorship spending. If you were selling a major sports concept, you'd be a fool to skip over these blue-chip names.

But you'd also be a fool if you ignored the flip side of these figures. If 17 per cent of this $4.3 billion market was concentrated among 20 companies, where was the remaining 83 per cent? The companies in this group might be harder to locate. They might have less generous budgets. They might be more selective in how they spent their cash. In other words, they might be harder sells. But they were well worth pursuing if you could match a company with the right idea.

I remember back in 1989 when one of our Cleveland sales executives, Jay Lotz, noticed that a company in New York named Snapple was launching a unique line of all-natural fruit beverages and bottled teas that tasted just like freshly brewed iced tea. The drinks were being marketed less for their taste and more for their all-natural, healthy, thirst-quenching qualities. In Lotz's mind that made Snapple a perfect candidate for a marketing tie-in with sports. So he scheduled a meeting at Snapple's 'world headquarters' in Woodside, Queens, about 30 minutes east of our Manhattan offices.

The drive to Snapple itself was a major achievement. Following Snapple's directions from Manhattan to Queens, Lotz found himself surrounded by a vast sea of warehouses in Woodside. The further Lotz drove, the more shabby the warehouses became until he made a final turn down a dead-end street. He stopped in front of a massive garbage dump. Next to the dump was another warehouse. A tiny sign on an industrial-strength steel door said 'Snapple Beverage Corp'. Lotz knocked on the door. A voice on the other side shouted, 'Who is it?'

Lotz identified himself and was shown into a caged reception area that reminded him more of a holding pen for prisoners than the standard corporate waiting room. From there Lotz was ushered into a cavernous room that the three middle-aged partners who had founded Snapple, Hyman Goldin, Arnold Greenberg, and Leonard Marsh, shared as an office.

The ambiance was not only low-rent but chaotic. Goldin's secretary disregarded his instruction to hold all calls by interrupting the meeting a half-dozen times. If Lotz was amused or discomfited by the unusual ambiance, he didn't let on. He couldn't help notice that the phones were ringing off the hook. As he went into his pitch about how using an athlete to endorse their product could jump-start Snapple's marketing efforts, he could see the partners eyes widen.

They were particularly interested in two tennis clients. The price tag, said Lotz, was somewhere between $350,000 and $500,000 per year, depending on how much of the client's time was needed.

One of the partners said, 'We'll pay $400,000 per year.'

Another partner interrupted, 'Why did you do that? You just told him how much money we have!'

Lotz was dumbfounded. These three men were fighting with each other in front of him! A part of him was thinking, 'There's no way these fellows have that kind of money. They're not credible.' Another part of him, though, remembered the phones ringing off the hook (always a good sign that business is booming). Lotz left the meeting elated, believing that he had unearthed a new customer who wanted to spend money.

What he didn't know at the time was that he had merely completed Phase 1 of the sale. He had sold Snapple on the idea of investing in sports. In Phase 2 he would have to sell the concept inside our company – because none of our clients would take Snapple's money.

Both tennis clients rejected the Snapple offer. The company was too small and unproven.

Lotz then suggested that Snapple become the official beverage of Universal Studios Florida, where we were in charge of selling corporate sponsorships. The Snapple partners loved the idea, but Universal wouldn't take their money. Again, they were dazzled by the blue chips. Snapple was an unknown quantity; it didn't have the right image.

The same thing happened with another amusement park where we were selling corporate sponsorships. Nobody wanted to take Snapple's money until the company was larger and more established.

Lotz didn't give up. He continued peppering Snapple *and* our clients with ideas until he scored with our client Ivan Lendl. Lendl already drank Snapple products, so he didn't need persuading. For their part, the Snapple partners loved Lendl's superfit image. It would be perfect for the new line of sport drinks they were developing. They also felt an affinity with Lendl. He had started out poor and worked his way to success, just like they had. Phase 2 ended happily with Lendl signing a lucrative three-year endorsement deal with Snapple.

Phase 3 is even more interesting, if only for what it says about the selling opportunities in little companies.

Snapple went on to become one of the great American entrepreneurial success stories of the 1990s. In 1994, five years after Lotz's initial call, the company was generating nearly one billion dollars in sales. It had a trend-setting advertising campaign that was becoming a classic case of how to build a brand name and image from ground zero. And its high-flying stock, at its peak, put the company's market value at more than $2 billion. The three Snapple partners were now wealthy men. Their company was no longer a tiny startup. It had money, credibility, and a desirable image.

There were two ironies to this development.

The first is that executives and clients at our company took notice of Snapple's success. Suddenly, Lotz began hearing that the same clients who had rejected Snapple a few years earlier were now eager to become involved with the company. In effect, they were saying, 'Get me a deal with Snapple.' Fortunately, Lotz had maintained a solid relationship with Snapple and was able to do more business with them. (This follows a cardinal selling rule: Your best customer is someone who has bought from you before.)

The second irony is that in November 1994 Snapple was acquired for $1.3 billion in cash by the Quaker Oats Company – number 13 on our top 20 list of blue-chip sports sponsors. Snapple is no longer one of a handful of rapidly growing companies. It is now a major part of one of our business's blue-chip customers – which represents another selling opportunity for us.

Yes, there's money to be made selling to the big

customers in your field. But don't put so much faith in your blue-chip customers that you ignore the giant opportunities your small customers represent. The small customers may reward your faith many times over.

The Seven Sins of Salesmanship (or What Makes My Customers Mad)

There are millions of customers and millions of specific reasons they get mad. But when all is said done, what makes customers mad falls into one of the following seven sins of salesmanship:

1   You don't deliver the product.

The first thing that makes a customer mad is the most obvious. You promise a certain product at a certain price within a certain time frame and don't deliver the product. This is obvious because in so many sales situations there are clear, objective criteria establishing exactly what the 'product' is. If the customer buys a 35-inch television, you don't deliver a 27-inch model.

But there are a lot of sales where the 'product' isn't so clearly defined. If we promise to create a tennis tournament for a sponsor, it has to be a good tournament – by the sponsor's standards, not ours. But who's to say what a 'good' tournament is? That's what makes delivering the product more tricky than it sounds. The first sin of selling is forgetting that you haven't delivered the product until the customer accepts it.

2   You don't deliver on price.

The second sin is failing to deliver on price. Again, if we promise to put on a tennis tournament for $500,000 and two-thirds down the line, because of unforeseen circumstances, we tell the customer that the original price is no longer valid and force him to pay more, the customer will be mad. I've never known a customer who enjoyed hearing his project was over budget.

3   You don't deliver on time.

Missing a deadline is the easiest way to enrage a customer – because deadlines are so unequivocal and so many people are counting on you to be on time. Just think how you feel when someone else keeps you waiting.

4   Two out of three is OK.

The fourth sin is thinking that, in terms of product, price, and time, achieving two out of three is all right. It isn't.

5   Selling and walking.

Another thing that makes a customer see red is when the salesperson disappears after making the sale.

I used to have this 'sell and walk' mentality in my youth – because I had no staff and I had to keep selling to keep the company going. But over the years, I realized that when a customer buys something from you, he's not just paying for a product. He's buying into a relationship with you. He wants you to stick around and 'hold his hand'. He wants you to ask him if everything is all right. He wants you to offer suggestions about how he can squeeze more benefits out of the product or service he has just purchased. He also wants to know if you have any ideas about other things he should be doing. In effect, he's inviting you to sell him something else. Forgetting that may be the biggest sin of all.

6   Ignoring the small details.

You can be doing the best job in the world for your customer in terms of product, pricing, and timing. But never think that gives you a license to ignore the small details of the sale.

For one thing, you can't predict what that small detail may be. What's minor to you may be major to the customer.

Secondly, with some customers, if you do 99 things right and one thing wrong, you can be sure they'll focus on that solitary error. That's human nature.

We once represented a golfer for whom, by any objective standard, we had done phenomenal work. We did everything from tripling his 'off the course' income to negotiating the sale of his old home and hiring an architect for his new one. We even advised his parents about their investments. These were services that went way beyond our standard obligations. One time, as he and his family went off for a European vacation, he asked someone in our office to book a rental car in Rome. For some reason, the reservation got lost and he was stranded at the Rome airport for three hours with a screaming baby and angry wife. His wife never stopped badgering him about how our company couldn't do anything right. That mishap, which was not our fault, poisoned a relationship at the precise moment it should have been peaking.

Customers with short memories are customers with short fuses.

7 Not knowing why they're mad

The other thing that makes customers mad is the fact that you don't know if and when they are mad. That usually means you're not as close to the customer as you should be – and that you're guilty of one or more of the first six sins.

Chapter 4
Perfecting Your Sales Technique

Don't Try to Control Factors Beyond Your Control

I used to think that the greatest frustration in sales was dealing with a prospect who wouldn't take my calls. But after a lifetime of selling, I've come to the conclusion that there's one greater exercise in futility: trying to control elements of the sale that are truly beyond your control.

In my particular field of sports, it took me some time to learn that I really didn't have much influence over critical factors such as:

- quality of the product
- public perception
- internal objections

Consider the first item, product quality. Our company's 'product' has always been athletes. We try to represent the best, under the theory that it's easier to sell a superstar's services than those of an also-ran (and the numbers tend to be bigger, too). But in the end, it's the athlete who establishes his or her level of quality by the performance on and off the field. We can take some of the distractions out of an athlete's life, but we can't control whether he or she wins championships. No matter how much we claim our client is the best, the proof is in the sports section of the customer's newspaper. It's beyond our control.

It's the same with public perception. No matter how

much spin control we try to exert to enhance a client's image, the press has the last word. It's beyond our control.

Likewise with internal objections. I've always been able to deal with a customer's objections face to face. But I've never known what to do about the objections voiced when I have left the room, when the customer takes my idea to his or her bosses and peers. That discussion is beyond my control.

If there is such a thing as wisdom in selling, it's being able to let go of the elements you cannot control and focusing instead on the elements you can. Consider these two:

1 Pace of the sale.

Salespeople are deluding themselves if they think they can speed up the timing of the customer's decision. Customers buy when they're ready to buy, not a moment sooner or later.

But salespeople can control one aspect of the sales process's pace. They can slow it down.

One of my proudest sales involved a golf concept and a Japanese company. From start to finish the sale took eight years, which is one reason I'm proud of it. During those eight years, there were any number of small ideas I could have sold to these Japanese executives in other sports. But numerous meetings with them suggested that they wanted to be involved in golf, and that when they got involved, they would do so in a big way.

The sales process took eight years because I took control of the pace. There were times when they actually wanted to buy into a concept and I said, 'No, this isn't right for you.' For the first seven years of our courtship, I couldn't exactly say what *was* right for them, but I knew what wasn't – and they trusted me. Finally, in Year 8, we came up with a sufficiently grand concept that made sense for them. By the time we closed the deal, it hardly seemed like a sale. They were so hungry to buy, it almost seemed as if we were presenting them with a gift.

I'm not sure it would have ended this way if I had let *them* control the pace.

2 The customer's anger.

I know a sales manager who claims he wakes up every morning and wonders which of his salespeople he should anger that day. He says, 'I want all my salespeople angry at me – for challenging them to do better, to call on more customers, to beat their quotas. If they're angry at me, maybe they'll take out some of that aggression on the customer.'

I'm not sure I'd want to be the sales manager inspiring all that hostility, but anger is an interesting factor in the buyer-seller relationship.

The fact is, all customers are angry about something. They might be angry about what a competitor is doing – and why they can't seem to match the competition move for move. They might be angry with their boss. They might be angry at their colleagues. They might be angry with their usual suppliers. A salesperson who can identify that anger – and control and assuage it – can sell anything.

Manipulating a customer's anger is risky; you're playing with fire. But sometimes the risk is worth it. Some years

ago I called on the CEO of an American company that had
made a huge investment in golf. Since I had known the
CEO for years, I couldn't believe he wasn't hiring our
company to help maximize this investment. Frankly, I was
a little angry with him. I felt betrayed.

When we met, I could see that he was feeling quite
pleased, if not smug, about his coup. So I decided to take a
few jabs at him, to get him a little angry. I told him that he
had wildly overspent on the project. I described how we
could have advised him on what other companies were
spending on comparable projects. As I went through the
various mistakes he had made, I could see his smugness
turning into rage, directed not at me but at himself and at
the subordinates who had negotiated the deal.

It was a risky maneuver, but with the CEO's temperature rising in front of me, it was relatively easy for me to
offer our services to help undo the damage and almost as
easy to get him to accept.

Putting Some Heat Into Your Cold Calls

Unless you're in a business where the phone is always
ringing, where the world is beating down your door to buy
your product or service, you have to make cold calls to sell.

I don't know anyone who will admit to enjoying the cold
call process. It's intrusive. It's fraught with rejection. It's
psychologically draining, especially if you're calling 100
people a day and 99 of them won't even agree to see you in
their office.

Here's a checklist of strategies that can put some heat
into your cold calls.

1   Have a pretext.

You need a reason for calling. It doesn't have to be a profound or persuasive reason, but it has to be slightly more compelling than, 'I want to sell you something.' That's not a pretext. That's a subtext – that is usually left unspoken.

One of my favorite pretexts, which I've been using for years, is to call someone when they have just started in a new job. The pretext could be nothing more than to congratulate them or welcome them to the community. But I'm not unmindful that a new executive in the first weeks on the job is (a) eager to make an impact (and therefore will be more receptive to ideas from the outside) and (b) has not been on the job long enough to become jaded and unresponsive to cold calls. This sort of information can be found in any local newspaper or trade publication, but I'm amazed how few people act on it.

2   Set modest goals.

Let's face it. You're not going to close a deal with one cold call. Selling doesn't work that way.

So you have to downsize your criteria for what makes a cold call a success. In our business, the goal is to get an appointment with the prospect so we can present our credentials. To some people, success can be as modest as getting past the prospect's secretary or getting him or her to say, 'Send me something in writing.' That's a first step. But without it, there is no second step.

It's a simple mental game. If you set humble, realistic

goals for your cold calls, you are more likely to consider them successes rather than dispiriting wastes of time.

3   Invite them to something.

This may be peculiar to our business, where we're involved with a lot of sporting events, but inviting people to a golf tournament or tennis match in their town is a great cold-call opener – and dramatically increases your chances of seeing the prospect again.

4   Aim high in the hierarchy.

As a general rule, it is better to cold call prospects near the top of the chain of command – and let them tell you how to work your way down – than to start out at the bottom thinking that you can work your way up.

In my experience, cold calling a junior person at a company can stall you at that low level for months – while the junior person tries to figure out who in the company has the authority to act on your idea. A senior person may not be overjoyed by your call, but he or she will quickly know who in the company you should be talking to.

5   Seek the decision-maker with tact.

On any cold call, you want to be dealing with the ultimate decision-maker, but it's hard to tell if you are. A lot of people think they can solve this problem by candidly asking the prospect, 'Are you the decision-maker on this?'

The problem with such candor, however, is that it rarely gets a frank or honest answer. Few people are willing to admit – either to themselves or to a stranger on the phone – that they are not decision-makers. Euphemisms like 'Am I speaking to the right person?' or 'Am I wasting your time with this?' are much warmer, less intrusive – and achieve the desired result.

6 Don't be too slick.

After making 50 calls a day, every day, it's perfectly understandable that your sales pitch will get more practiced and more polished. But there's a fine line between sounding well-rehearsed and sounding slick. Well-rehearsed means you know what you're talking about but can make it sound as if you are saying it for the first time. Slick means that you are reciting your lines or you're impatient to get to the next call or you're bored. If you feel that way, how do you think the person on the other end of the line feels?

7 Find a friendly ear.

A wag in our marketing group once advised our young salespeople to avoid cold calling the marketing director at a company. 'The marketing guys are flooded with calls and proposals,' he said. 'You're much better off calling the public relations guy. He's paid to listen and be enthusiastic. And he'll point you in the right direction.' Beneath the cynicism, there's some truth in this remark. Every company has friendly, receptive people who listen with their ears rather than their lips. They can frequently be found in line divisions with names like Public Affairs or Investor Relations or Human Resources or even Legal Affairs. They may not have a budget to buy anything from you, but they often can pinpoint exactly who does have the budget.

Questions That Should Be in Every Salesperson's Sample Case

The basic tenets of salesmanship are eternal. You still have to know your product, know yourself, know your customers, and when in doubt, rely on common sense.

But if like me, you've been out selling in the marketplace in recent years, it will be obvious to you that the sales climate has radically changed. Customers are more sophisticated. They know when they are being 'sold'. They're better informed about their buying needs. They have many more buying options – and instant access to data on these alternatives. They're harder to reach. And when you reach them, they don't have enough time to hear your story.

Here is a checklist of questions that, properly addressed, can improve your sales success in the immediate future.

1 Are you selling or are you marketing?

This is what I mean by customers who know when they are being 'sold'.

Selling is the process of persuading the customer to buy because it satisfies your needs – i.e., so you can meet a quarterly sales quota or unload expensive inventory or keep your boss off your back. Marketing, by contrast, is the process of finding out customers' needs and then persuading them that your product or service legitimately meets their needs. Guess which strategy customers prefer?

2 Have you budgeted time to listen?

Every salesperson recognizes the importance of listening to the customer. It is timeless advice. But not enough people practise it, perhaps because they don't know how.

Most salespeople are so intent on perfecting their sales presentation and projecting themselves as knowledgeable and confident that they forget the customer needs to do a little projecting as well. The best way to listen to the customer is to make time for it – and lock it in.

As you prepare for your next sales call, fine-tuning your proposal and calibrating your talk down to minutes and seconds, ask yourself: Have I budgeted time to listen? More important, have I budgeted considerably more time for the customer to talk than for myself?

3 Is your proposal short enough?

Customers are no longer impressed by – nor do they have the time to read – lengthy proposals. In fact, the most savvy customers regard an overwrought proposal as a sign that you don't know what you're talking about. The best concepts can be expressed in one or two sentences and can inspire the customer's commitment on the spot. If you measure your proposals by how much they weigh rather than what they say, perhaps you need to rethink them.

4 Have you price-conditioned the customer?

Before a customer can accept your price, he must be prepared to hear it. You never want to quote a price that exceeds the one the customer has in mind.

You must first establish your price by pre-conditioning the customer – by citing examples of what other customers have done at a given price level. Choose your examples with care and the customer may raise his sights to meet your expectations.

5 Have you let them say 'No' lately?

No customer wants to be regarded as a pushover, as someone who'll say yes to anything you suggest. Customers have a need to say no – to maintain their dignity and the sense that they are in control. So let them.

If you have one concept you're trying to sell, you're much better off prefacing your strong idea with a few bad ones. Once he's had a chance to dismiss your dumb ideas, even the flintiest of customers will be predisposed to accept a good one.

6 Can you say 'No' even when the customer says 'Yes'?

Salespeople, by training, are rarely prepared to 'unsell' their product or service, especially in the face of a customer who desperately wants to buy. But if you can honestly tell a customer 'I don't think this is right for you. Why don't we put it off for another time,' the rewards can be extraordinary. You may have lost the customer's order but you will have gained something far more valuable – the customer's trust.

7 Are you selling one on one?

For some reason, salespeople think that a sales call increases in importance by how many unfamiliar faces are in attendance. Not true. The only thing that increases is the degree of difficulty in getting the order. By definition, it's easier to persuade one person rather than two, two rather than three, and so on, because with each additional person you have to overcome a multiplicity of interests and cross-purposes.

If you're constantly making sales presentations to committees, you have only yourself to blame. Once you find the right individual at a company, insist on meeting him (or her) one on one. If he likes your concept, he'll find a way to sell it to his colleagues.

8 How well do you know the customer's competition?

Preferably, you know the customer's competition better than he does. Few things in business are more impressive than a salesperson who not only tells me what I should be buying but why and how it will give me an edge over my competitors.

If you want to convince your customers that you are their 'partner' rather than 'a vendor', teaming up with them against their competition is a great place to start.

9 Do you still fear failure?

I've been selling for 30 years and I still feel a flicker of fear before each call. Fear of rejection. Fear of failure. It's the greatest motivator I know.

If you don't feel a twinge of fear before a major sales push, perhaps you aren't putting enough of yourself into the effort.

Questions to Keep You on Your Toes *During* the Sale

The trouble with selling is that it is such a fragile process. Until you have the money in hand, there's always something that can go wrong. Circumstances change. The customer changes his mind. You do something to lose the customer's trust.

You have to be on your toes every step of the way because the slightest miscue can sabotage a process that may have taken months to assemble.

Here is a checklist of questions you should be asking yourself at every stage of the sales process with every customer.

1 Have you promised the moon lately?

Promising what you can't deliver is a common selling trap – because it's so easy to fall into. In the heat of a sale, as salesman and customer spark ideas and get excited about the possibilities of working together, it's not unusual for people to overextend themselves and promise the moon.

But where will you be when it's time to deliver and the customer feels that you've failed? You've made a sale but lost a customer.

2   Can you arrest the urge for instant gratification?

All of us are pulled by the urge for instant gratification. And the pressures of selling only compound this feeling. Once a salesman believes he can make people buy *what* he wants them to buy, it's not too long before he believes he can also get them to buy *when* he wants them to buy.

That's a dangerous delusion. People and events tend to move at their own pace and rarely bother to synchronize with your timetable.

I suspect more deals fall apart because of impatience, the urge for instant gratification, than for almost any other reason. If you can harness this urge and tailor your timing to suit the buyer's timetable, you will save many more sales than you lose.

3   Have you noticed their new suit?

People, despite their protestations, like it when you compliment them on a change in their appearance – a slimmer waistline, a new haircut, a new suit. It not only marks you as an attentive person, but it confirms in their mind that the change was a wise one.

The same thing happens in sales. Industries shift. Companies reorganize. Customers change. And it's a very gratifying feeling for customers when you notice that their buying needs are different. It marks you as a sensitive business person, and reminds customers why they bought from you in the first place.

4 Are you seen on the street?

One of the dangers of being a good salesperson is that your customers won't let you keep on selling. That's because once you make a sale, you also have to implement it. Servicing the account forces you into the office, away from other potential customers.

An executive at another company told me the other day, 'I always know where to find Jim, my best salesman. He's in the office. He has sold so much to his three biggest accounts that tending to the details takes up all his time. I wish he was back on the street selling.'

It's always a good idea to ask yourself, 'Are you selling? Or servicing an account?' Both are important jobs. But which one makes more sense for you and your customers?

5 How deep is your agenda?

I'm a big believer in never leaving a sales meeting without selling something. If I can't sell a customer the high-ticket project at the top of my agenda, I'll try something from the less expensive end of the list. If nothing else, it means our time wasn't a complete waste. More important, I've started a new relationship that could lead to future sales.

I am continuously reminding people in our organization to have more than one item on their sales agenda. I don't want them to be so tunnel-visioned that they accept the customer's response on one issue and leave it at that. Tunnel-vision – the belief that you call on someone only to sell them what you need to sell or what they think you came to sell – is one of the most pernicious fallacies of selling.

6   Are you selling to the right person?

Sometimes during a sale, the nature of the deal changes so completely that you find you're talking to the wrong person. It's important every once in a while, especially in a complicated transaction that goes on for months, to look around and check out the cast of characters. Your 'contact' may no longer be the appropriate decision maker.

We noticed this recently with an automobile company that was introducing a new model and wanted it to be identified with a major sport. For months we had bombarded a senior vice president at the automaker's advertising agency with proposals – to no avail. Yet the senior VP continued to encourage us.

Then one day, while discussing an unrelated matter, a friend at the auto company informed us that we were talking to the wrong person. Sports promotion had been taken in-house at the automaker. And the senior VP, whose ego may have been bruised, didn't have the heart or nerve to tell us.

I'm told we will make a sale shortly, but I'd sleep better at night knowing we had identified the right decision-maker on our own rather than through the fortuitous suggestion of a friend.

How to Put More Power Into Your Powerful Ideas

It is one thing to come up with a brilliant idea. Making it practical and bringing it to fruition is an achievement of an entirely different order. Here are two simple strategies that will make your powerful idea more palatable to people who are more inclined to resist an idea than embrace it.

1 Hook it up to another engine.

I think so many good ideas go astray because people neglect to make them practical. It's as if they feel that their job is simply to present an idea – the more clever it is, the more 'blue sky' it contains the better – and then bask in the applause for displaying such a bold, fertile imagination. The real job of getting the idea accepted, funded, and implemented is practically an afterthought.

I try not to indulge in this ego tripping – and I don't know many successful people who do either. After all, which would you rather be? The architect whose drawings win raves, or the one whose designs get built?

The easiest way to add a little more horsepower to a good idea is to hook it up to someone else's engine. In our company that means tailoring an idea so that it exploits our already existing resources.

For example, a few months ago someone in our publishing division had an idea for a tennis instruction book. The idea didn't get very far. (Frankly, it wasn't that unique. There is a glut of tennis instructionals.)

But a few weeks later a simple twist resurrected the idea into a winner. The originator suggested publishing the book as the 'official training manual' of one of our clients, a major tennis federation.

Suddenly, the idea made practical sense for all concerned. The tennis federation was delighted to have an 'official' book and planned to distribute thousands of copies. The publishers increased their funding when they saw how many copies were pre-sold. As for us, the idea was a double dip. Not only had we made a commercial idea more viable, but we had solidified a relationship with an important client.

2   Push the good with the bad.

A good idea looks even better when it is preceded or followed by a bad one.

I don't say this as an endorsement of bad ideas. But consider the following situation.

People are quite often asked to present a shopping list of ideas in a meeting. They'll have 20 ideas jotted down on a piece of paper – ideas that presumably they have given a lot of thought to.

And yet it amazes me how little thought they give to the order in which they present these ideas.

Most people follow the obvious pattern of ranking their ideas in order of descending merit. They start off with their strongest idea and work their way down the list. The big problem with this, of course, is that your grand finale is your weakest idea!

A standup comic doesn't close his act with his weakest joke. Neither should you. Pay attention to the order in which you present your ideas – and give your audience time to digest what you are saying.

If you have 24 ideas, no one expects all of them to be of equal brilliance. So pace yourself. Start out with a strong idea to pique everyone's interest and establish your credibility. Then go to a few marginal ideas, and then come back with a good one. And so on.

If you organize your thoughts properly, the good ideas will stand out like diamonds, and no one will care about the bad ones (because they will be forgotten).

What Salespeople Can Learn from a Sommelier

I never cease to marvel at the sales skills of a great wine steward or sommelier at a top restaurant. Quite often, particularly when one of them has persuaded me to spend $60 on a bottle of wine when I intended to spend $30, I'm convinced that wine stewards are the most accomplished salespeople in the world.

Think of all the obstacles they must overcome to ring up a sale.

For one thing, a bottle of wine is not a 'must have' when you dine out. Many people prefer hard liquor or beer or soda with their meal.

Nor is wine an impulse buy. Quite often, wine is a collective decision. You have to get everyone at the table to agree on red or white, sweet or dry, inexpensive or pricey.

Then there's the knowledge gap, the anxiety of buying the 'right' bottle. When it comes to wine, most of us are uneducated consumers. We really don't know what we're buying.

Perhaps the biggest obstacle is the markup. Unlike buying a car or a sweater or a book, where you have a pretty good idea of the manufacturer's suggested list price, buying a bottle of wine in a restaurant can be a tremendous extravagance. It is one of those rare experiences where you can be sure you will be paying at least twice what you would pay at retail!

How, in this uneasy and suspicious climate, does a sommelier make a sale?

By exercising restraint.

At the top restaurants, the best sommeliers are masters at winning a customer's trust. They realize the customer's anxiety about wine and they allay it rather than play on it. If you don't want wine, they don't try to change your mind. If you do, they will educate you. If you ask for a recommendation, they will come up with a wine that makes sense, usually from the middle of the list. At a less scrupulous establishment, they might hustle you with a wine from the top of the list.

You also see this restraint in how the wine is served. The top sommeliers will pour the wine halfway in a glass, letting you nourish and enjoy it. Then they refill it halfway. They don't hustle you by filling and refilling your glass to the top so you order another bottle.

It's no different in any other line of business. The salesperson in the clothing store who can honestly tell you, 'No, that $800 coat isn't right for you. This $400 coat is much better,' knows this instinctively.

The best salespeople realize that winning the customer's trust, even during an encounter that lasts only a few minutes, is usually a matter of exercising restraint. They know that the customer has certain preconceptions and limits, and that they're better off coming in under those limits rather than exceeding them.

Try it the next time a customer suggests a transaction that you know is wrong for them. When every fibre of your being cries out to close the easy sale, just say no. You may lose out on a quick hit. The customer may walk out the door. But he will leave with a great feeling about you – and definitely come back for more.

Knowing When the 'Buy' Decision Is Really Made

Some years ago on a Cleveland-to-Denver flight I was seated next to a talkative sales executive from a computer services company. In the course of our conversation, the young man started extolling the talents of his company's CEO and how he had doubled the company's sales every year for the last four years.

I told the young man, 'Your boss sounds like a terrific salesman. I hope you're learning a lot from him.'

The young man corrected me with a fascinating insight. 'Actually, if you spent some time with him you'd never know he sells for a living,' he said. 'He's shy and pretty dull as a speaker. I've been to meetings with him when he's hardly said a word. His secret weapon is an incredible sense of timing. He'll tell one of our salespeople something like, 'I think it's time you called again on this or that customer and invariably it turns out the customer is very interested. A tiny suggestion becomes a great sales lead. If he has a skill it seems to be an uncanny knack for knowing when people want to buy. I'm not sure if you can teach that.'

Neither was I, but the young sales executive was already ahead of the crowd simply by recognizing that knowing when the customer makes the 'buy' decision is an important part of knowing how to sell.

Basically, there are only three times when customers make 'buy' decisions:
- Before you walk into the room.
- While you're in the room.
- After you leave the room.

Effective salespeople are always on the lookout for clues about which category applies to them – and they know how to seize the moment rather than kill it. Here are some lessons I've learned over the years about when the 'buy' decision is made.

1 Before you walk into the room.

Theoretically, this is the ideal situation – a customer who's already made up his mind. He has an intense need (or lust) to buy whatever you're selling. All you have to do is step out of the customer's way and not say or do anything to undo the sale. This situation is more common than you think.

I remember calling on a newspaper syndicate in my younger days when I was trying to interest them in running a weekly strip of golf tips. The syndicate chief was incredibly friendly to me as he showed me into his office. I wasn't accustomed to such civility. In those days, I often had to fight my way into companies to explain the concept of marketing through sports to indifferent and sometimes hostile audiences. But this chief was so polite, I was caught speechless. So I let him talk.

It soon became obvious that he had decided to buy my golf instructional strip before I ever showed up. It turned out that twice a year – in Autumn and Spring – his syndicate launched four new features. He had three features in hand, but he was desperate for a fourth to fill out his portfolio. He was hoping the fourth would be our golf strip.

I learned a lot from that meeting, not the least of which was to keep my mouth shut if the other guy wanted to talk. But the big lesson was about timing. For several years thereafter, we always made a point of calling the syndicate chief just before his Autumn and Spring selling season – when his interest was most keen.

In almost every field, there are certain slots in the calendar year when customers are more willing (if not downright eager) to buy. If you can pin down these time periods, don't be surprised if the customer has made the 'buy' decision before you walk through the door.

2   While you're in the room.

This is the trickiest buy to spot – because many salespeople are so engrossed in making their sales pitch, they don't notice when their pitch has worked. Unless the customer says, 'Stop! Where do I sign?' they keep talking.

An executive at an industrial supply company once explained to me how easily this can happen. A salesman for the Yellow Pages business-to-business telephone directory tried to convince him to advertise in his directory.

'He struck me as a buttoned-up salesman at first. He had a complete history of our ad spending in the Yellow Pages. He had the page marked in the last edition we advertised in. He wanted to know why we stopped advertising.

'So I told him there were a couple of reasons.

'But before I could list them, he interrupted me. "I can give you five reasons," he said. "First, you've been in business 35 years so people already know who you are. Second, you have a sales force; reaching new customers is their job. Third, the Yellow Pages just reaches annoying customers who take hours of your time and then only buy $100 of material. Fourth, . . ."

'I couldn't believe my ears. I started out with two reasons not to buy and this guy was giving me three more reasons I never thought of!

'Then he opened up the directory and showed me where my ad used to run. I looked at the page and in the bottom left-hand corner I noticed a tiny ad selling an obscure brand of equipment which, it so happened, I had been trying to track down for weeks. To me, this was the most incredible form of serendipity and I mentioned it to the salesman. If there was any reason to place an ad, here was proof that his Yellow Pages worked.

'I was so pleased, I think if he had taken out his order book and asked me to buy, I would have done so on the spot. But he never asked.'

Persuading a customer to buy the first time you meet is not a common event. When it happens, don't let the moment pass you by.

3   After you leave the room.

This is how most 'buy' decisions are made – after you're gone and the customer has time to reflect or consult his boss or associates. The good news is that the customer usually tells you that he will decide in the near future ('Call me in two weeks about this after we've had a chance to study your proposal.') The bad news is that you don't know what unseen forces or people are influencing that buy decision for or against you while you're waiting.

I don't think people take full advantage of this waiting period between the initial sales call and the call back for a decision. Other than sending the standard follow-up letter ('Thanks for seeing me. If there's anything else I can do, please feel free to call . . .'), most people simply move on to other things.

My strategy has always been to do everything I can to impress the prospect. If he tells me to call back in a week, I would ask for a specific time that's most convenient for him – and then I call precisely at the designated time. If nothing else, it says something about my precision. I also would send the prospect pertinent newspaper clips and documents that might amplify our proposal – anything to keep the concept near the front of his mind. Most important, I would work very hard to identify the unseen people who are influencing the decision – and make them see my point of view.

One of our executives recently met with the CEO of a beverage company about a sports sponsorship concept. The CEO liked the concept and called in his marketing vice president for a second opinion (sometimes a good sign, but not always). The marketing VP listened to our executive repeat his pitch, asked a few questions, and then walked out, saying, 'I've heard enough. I think I understand what you're proposing.'

The meeting ended a few minutes later with the CEO suggesting that we call back in ten days. Ten days later, when our executive called, the CEO told him, 'We haven't made up our minds. Some people here like the idea. A couple of people aren't sure they understand it.'

Figuring that the CEO wouldn't give the green light to

the idea without his marketing VP's support, our executive inquired who at the company was undecided.

The CEO was slightly coy. 'Actually, you met one of them when you were here,' he said.

'Would it help if I met with him,' our executive asked.

'I can't see how it would hurt,' the CEO said.

Armed with the CEO's blessing, our executive arranged a meeting with the VP, cleared up a lot of issues, and soon closed the sale.

I'm not sure we would have achieved the same result if our executive didn't appreciate that the 'buy' decision could go either way once he left the room.

Three Good Reasons to Depart from the Script

Part of what makes a great quarterback in football is his ability to call 'audibles'. Ordinarily, the quarterback calls the next offensive play in the huddle. But when he lines up above the center and sees a defense perfectly arranged to stop the play, he'll call an audible. There at the line of scrimmage, with only a handful of seconds to snap the ball, he'll shout out a new play to his teammates that has a better chance of working. If the defense is stacked up to stop the run up the middle he had originally called, he may switch to a quick pass to a wide receiver.

Audibles are a subtle part of a football game, but they often represent the margin between victory and defeat. A quarterback needs instinct and confidence to call them.

I wish more people had the same instinct and confidence when they conduct business meetings. One of the biggest reasons so many of us complain about meetings is that the people running them are prisoners of their agenda. You can't fault people for preparing for a meeting or sales call, for having an itemized agenda of all the points they want to cover. But it is dangerous to ignore the circumstances of the meeting itself – the people, the mood, the timing – in an effort to stick to that agenda. That's when calling an audible can be the smartest play of all.

Of course, before you abandon your carefully prepared agenda, you have to recognize the circumstances that are working against it. Whenever I walk into a meeting, I'm always looking for clues that tell me whether my set plays will work – and whether I need to alter my plans.

Clue 1. Too many people.

I usually have a good idea of how many people should be in a meeting and when that number is too large to be productive. In a sales meeting, my ideal number is two (the customer and I), because I can sell best one on one. If the size of the meeting gets unwieldy for me, I won't plow through my agenda. Instead, I'll call an audible that reduces the number.

I learned this years ago when I arranged what I thought was a private meeting with the head of a television network. When I walked into the meeting, however, I was greeted by him and a half-dozen of his subordinates. I didn't think it would be a problem, but it was obvious after a few minutes that the subordinates were so busy trying to impress the boss with self-serving comments and interruptions, that nothing substantive was going to happen at this meeting. I abandoned my sales pitch and made a quick but graceful retreat. The next day I called the network chief back and suggested we meet alone. He laughed, apologized for his unruly staffers, and agreed to see me. He was an expert at meeting dynamics and knew exactly what I was after.

If your meeting is too crowded, don't fool yourself into thinking you can tame the crowd. You're better off waiting for another day, when the crowd has vanished and your voice can be more clearly heard.

Clue 2. No one is prepared.

I remember a college professor who simply dismissed the class when he realized no one had read that day's assignment. He didn't chide or lecture us. But in his own mild way he shamed us for not being prepared. The message was clear: He wasn't going to deliver his prepared lecture to people who weren't prepared to appreciate it. I doubt if any of us ever came to his class again with the assignment unread.

The same tactic applies in a business meeting. If the people in your meeting have not done their homework, don't think you'll accomplish much by forcing through your agenda. You may make a more lasting impression by ending the meeting and telling the attendees to use the remaining time to get prepared.

This dramatic gesture is a little harder to pull off with customers. Like most people, I've made sales calls on prospects who had no idea who I was and certainly hadn't read any of the carefully prepared materials I had sent before the meeting. It would be nice to be able to walk out on such rude behavior. But where some people see an insult, I see an opportunity. The prospect's ignorance is an opening to educate him. Instead of taking umbrage at the rude treatment, I turn very conciliatory. I take them to Page One and tell them all about myself and what our company can do. Customers tend to be so surprised by this tactic they often let me stay longer than scheduled – and many of them end up buying from us.

Clue 3. Not enough time.

One of our executives was recently competing with three other firms for a huge assignment with a major packaged goods company. The decision would be made after a one-day marathon review process in which each firm made a two-hour presentation to the company's top marketing executives. We were scheduled last.

By the time our executive's turn came, the review was running an hour behind schedule. Our executive was well prepared. He had sprinkled his presentation with comments that showed he knew everything about the company and its top management. But it only took a few minutes to see that the top decision-maker in the room was in a hurry. That was obvious when he cut off the usual small talk that opens these sessions and said, 'Let's get on with it.'

So our executive called an audible. He abandoned the prepared script and said, 'Look, I was ready to talk for an hour about our credentials. But you know who we are and what we can do. So why don't I save all of us some time and give you our best idea. If you want to know more after that, I'll be happy to stay.'

It was a gutsy call. But boring an impatient prospect with the prepared two-hour script was probably riskier.

(Fortunately, they liked our best idea and threw the business our way.)

If you need more time to present your case than the prospect is prepared to give, you won't impress him by sticking to the routine; actually, you'll be overstaying your welcome. It's more impressive if you can refit your remarks to the time allotted. It's even more impressive if you can make your case in less time than the prospect has given. If you give people the gift of time (and let them know why you're doing so), they will never resent you for it.

On Becoming Well Informed

In 1991 I had an extraordinary no-holds-barred meeting with several division managers of Chrysler Motors. Automobile companies tend to take large sponsorship positions in various sports and our company has a number of ongoing projects with Chrysler's various divisions. So I asked for the meeting as a temperature reading on an important relationship.

It wasn't a pretty sight.

They went through a laundry list of complaints about us – everything from stories about one of our athlete clients who was actively badmouthing the sports program they were sponsoring to the 'sell and walk' mentality of one of our divisions. They described in great detail how accessible our executives had been in selling a concept to them and how unreachable they became when it came to executing the concept.

They had a nice laugh at my expense about all the sales proposals our salespeople had sent them in the last 12 months, not one of which addressed their primary goal of timing a sports sponsorship with the new products they would be launching in 1992 and 1993. 'Mark,' they said, 'your people have no idea how to sell to us.'

In fairness, they had some nice things to say about other parts of our company. But I walked out of that conference room with some serious bruises.

Yet it was a remarkable meeting – because it gave me information, the kind of information that I needed and that customers are rarely willing to give. What could be better than a customer honestly levelling with you?

Unfortunately, that's not usually the case. Customers tend to be very wary of sharing too much information with the salespeople who call on them, perhaps because they think the salesperson will use that information as a negotiating tool against them.

In my ideal world all customers would be as blunt and forthcoming as the executives from Chrysler. They would not only tell me what I was doing right and wrong, but they would map out all their buying needs for me. They would teach me how they wanted to be sold. The following strategies can help achieve that ideal state.

1   Candor begets candor.

There's a mimicking process in every dialogue. If I start out a meeting talking softly and politely, chances are the other side, consciously or not, will pick up my verbal cues and talk softly and politely. Likewise, if I'm loud and confrontational, the other side will probably be equally aggressive.

Thus, if you want total candor from a customer, you

should be prepared to be totally candid yourself. Quite often, I have gone into a customer's office with the specific intention of being as frontal as business decorum allows. It's not that I want to offend the customer. It's simply the only way to get him to open up.

For example, I once called on a very good customer who was doing business with one of our competitors. There's nothing wrong with customers buying from other suppliers. That's their prerogative. But it bothered me. I wanted to know what we were doing wrong that forced him to turn to someone else.

I could have asked him politely, but he probably would have given a polite, meaningless answer. Instead, I was candid. I told him he had drastically overpaid in one of the transactions and that we would never have asked him to agree to some of the terms our competitor had forced on him. In so many words I accused him of being an amateur. My verbal onslaught had the desired effect. He didn't back down. He defended his decision point by point with equal candor, in the course of which he told me his company's long-term goals, marketing strategies, and the hot buttons that make his people buy.

I suppose he thought he was putting me in my place. He was really putting me in the know.

2   People love to talk about themselves. Let them.

Getting information, of course, doesn't usually require such premeditated hostility. More often than not, the smartest premeditated tactic is being polite and willing to listen. (Note: This is the fourth time I've mentioned the power of listening. It cannot be stressed too often.)

I've known executives who, before a sales call, literally budget two minutes of a meeting to talk about their company and 20 minutes for the customer to talk about theirs. This tactic doesn't lead to a very balanced discussion. But very few customers seem to notice.

Most people can't wait to tell you how well they are doing. So don't make them wait.

3   Give a little in return.

Getting information is not a one-way street. At some point, even the most guileless and talkative customer will feel he's giving away too much. To become well informed, you have to inform the other side too.

Ideally, your information should sound like it's 'confidential' even when it's not. I often go into a negotiation armed with a few bulletins that I can afford to give away – because, like anyone else, I have certain proprietary information that I take for granted which another party might be dying to know. After I've shared my secrets, it's pretty difficult for them to keep theirs.

4   Test your source's authority.

As important as getting information may be, it's meaningless if you don't know how to determine its reliability. Some people, intentionally or not, simply tell you things that are wrong.

I like to test a source's authority early on by asking questions I already know the answers to. It's not foolproof, but if the other party is wrong I at least have identified someone who is either wasting my time or needs my help more than he knows.

I also like to repeat questions at subsequent meetings. The contradictions, if they come up, speak volumes about the reliability of the person supplying the answers.

Chapter 5
Making Your Sales Style
Work for You

A CEO once described the selling style of one of his best salespeople. He calls this salesman's style the 'Columbo', after the American television detective played by Peter Falk, whose rumpled raincoat and bumbling, addle-brained investigative methods conceal a shrewd mind that always traps the criminal and closes the case. According to the CEO, this top salesman operates like Columbo – and he's just as successful.

'I should have seen it when I interviewed him for the job,' the CEO told me. 'The first impression he made was horrible. His tie was askew. He was nervous and perspiring. He bumped into the furniture, fumbled with his briefcase, and almost knocked over my desk lamp. It was comical.

'But there was something about him that was intriguing. Every once in a while during our conversation, just when I was ready to write him off, he'd come out with an interesting insight or put me on the spot with a tough question that I had never heard before. There was more to him than met the eye.

'I invited my chief financial officer to meet him, and he had the same impression. This fellow's packaging may have been unorthodox, but he caught your attention and he made you think. So we hired him.'

According to the CEO this 'Columbo' sells the same way

he interviewed for the job. Prospects take one look at him when he walks into their office and immediately underestimate him. But as he sits there listening to them and asking probing questions and pitching ideas for their consideration, they begin to adjust their opinion of him – invariably upwards. By the time the meeting is over, quite often he's turned them around 180 degrees; they've come to like and respect him. In that frame of mind, they are even ready and willing to buy from him. That's when he pounces.

Some of his best sales have been made as the meeting ends and he is walking out the prospect's door. Then, as if hit by a flash of inspiration, he turns around to say, 'One other thing. It just occurred to me that we have a new product that might fit in with what you were saying about. . . .'

Clearly, this approach would not work for everybody. Few of us could affect the manner of an absent-minded professor, and even fewer of us could make it work to our advantage.

I think every salesperson, for better or worse, has a distinct selling style. The most successful salespeople are the ones who are aware of their style. They've consciously honed and perfected a modus operandi that meshes with their personality and doesn't conflict with the product or service they are selling. They know exactly what they're doing.

Do you?

Here are five sales styles that may work (or may already be working) for you:

1 The Wind-Up Doll

Some people's selling secret is simply to cover more ground than anyone else. Like a wind-up doll, they are in constant motion. They hit as many prospects as time allows, on the theory that throwing a case of darts at your target increases the chance of scoring a bullseye. There's nothing wrong with this. Sometimes you will be in a sales situation where your product or service is not appreciably different or better than that of your competition. That's when this sales style works best. What distinguishes you from the crowd is your energy and enthusiasm. If you can't out-think or out-talk the competition, why not outrun them?

2 The Human Backboard

In the 1970s, tennis player Harold Solomon was known as 'The Human Backboard' because of his ability and willingness to stay on the baseline for hours and return virtually any shot his opponent could muster. This was Solomon's consciously chosen style of play. He knew that, more often than not, he could outlast more talented opponents by simply keeping the ball in play – and waiting for them to make an error. This endurance test wasn't always pretty to watch, but it made Solomon far more successful than many people would have predicted.

Like Solomon, some salespeople are human backboards. They can take almost any shot, any negative, any form of rejection and hit it back to their advantage. They know that staying in the game is often more important than hitting an outright winner.

A few years back one of the most effective salesmen I know called on a major telecommunications company to interest them in sports sponsorship. The meeting did not get off to a good start. In fact, after hearing the salesman's pitch, the company's marketing chief tore into him with a scathing critique.

'I have heard a lot about your company, that you're overpriced and underinformed,' he said. 'And everything you've said thus far confirms that. Your remarks have shown me that you have no idea what our company is all about, what our marketing objectives are, who our customers are, and how our people operate. . . .'

The salesman endured this tirade for several more minutes. When the marketing chief finished, the salesman rose to his feet, smashed the marketing chief's desk with his fist, and said, 'That's exactly what I'm talking about. We don't know what you want. Why don't you tell us?'

In other words, he was a human backboard. He hit the shot right back at him.

The marketing chief had not expected this response. In fact, he was so stunned that he did as he was asked. He invited the salesman to sit down and spent the next two hours telling him exactly how to sell to his company.

3 The Voice

I'll never forget the first time I heard the American broadcaster Walter Cronkite speak in person. His voice was so deep and resonant and seductive that it almost overshadowed what he had to say. It was a pleasure to hear him (as well as to listen to him) and helped explain why Cronkite had stayed on top so long as CBS News' anchorman. Without denigrating his considerable journalistic skills, I think Cronkite's voice was an integral part of his ability to 'sell' the news to America. And I suspect he knew it.

Not every salesperson, of course, is blessed with great vocal cords. But some of the most effective salespeople I know are people who can create any mood they desire by the way they color, inflect and modulate their voice.

Capitalizing on the enormous color range of the human voice is not a sales style that many people adopt or are even aware of. But that fact alone should make it more valuable to you.

Think about this the next time you prepare for a sales call: As you rehearse your lines, decide how you want to appear. Do you want to appear strong and in control? Well-informed? Confident? Confiding? Curious? Eager? Combative? Desperate? Indifferent? All of these can be conveyed through your voice.

4 The Joker

Humor is the most valuable sales tool, because it is the quickest way to get people to like you, and when people like you they are more likely to buy from you. But humor is also the most dangerous sales tool, because you can never be sure what makes people laugh. What tickles one prospect can infuriate another.

All of us, I'm sure, have met people who are simply not funny. Yet have you ever heard someone admit that they don't have a sense of humor?

The fact is, some people are funny. Most people aren't. Before you make humor a significant part of your selling style, ask a friend or a customer if you are in the first group or the latter.

5   The Expert

Some effective salespeople have virtually no sales style at all – at least not in the cosmetic sense that we normally associate with supersalespeople. Their style is their knowledge and their expertise – which brings me to the paradox that . . .

Some of the Best Salespeople I Know Think They 'Don't Know How to Sell'

In recent years several friends and associates have commented to me that they 'don't know how to sell'. Yet in my opinion they are among the best salespeople I know.

One is a publishing executive who has had a long, distinguished career. In almost any business situation, he is usually perceived as the smartest person in the room. He projects authority because he is knowledgeable. Because of that, people not only listen to what he has to say, but they believe it and are willing to buy into it.

Another produces documentary films. I've heard him mumble that he's not a salesman, that he'd rather be behind the camera. But in front of prospective investors, I've seen him describe a project with such obvious enthusiasm and love for the material that few people can resist his 'pitch'.

Neither of these individuals has the outward trappings that we normally associate with salesmanship – the smooth line, the mellifluous voice, the brash demeanor, and the self-confidence that they can sell ice cubes to Eskimos. But still they are 'salespeople' because they possess the most important quality of salesmanship. Unwittingly or not, they can make other people want to buy.

Keep this in mind the next time you find yourself doubting your sales aptitude. You probably have more going for you than you realize.

Don't underrate knowledge

Your most underrated asset, of course, is knowledge. If you know your subject cold, you're automatically one up on everyone else in the room. They literally have to look to you for answers and quite often they will be willing to pay for that.

We have an executive in our corporate marketing group who I know does not position himself as a salesman. He thinks of himself as an information gatherer who advises a corporate client after one of our 'salespeople' has sold that company on our services.

Yet if you look over his achievements in recent years and the revenues he generates, it's clear that he's quite a salesman. I've seen him get up in a sales presentation with his charts and slides and cover a topic so thoroughly that the other side begins to see connections and possibilities they never knew existed. This is the best and most lasting kind of salesmanship. He doesn't have to persuade people to buy. Instead, his expertise so thoroughly reorients their thinking that they persuade themselves.

Sell your reputation

Another undervalued asset is your reputation. I know an award-winning magazine editor whose prestige favorably colors almost every meeting he attends. Like many editorial types, he's very low key and shy. He's more interested in words and pictures than in manipulating people. But that concentration and his years of being right far more often than he is wrong make him a very effective salesman when publishers seek his opinion on writers or story ideas. His editorial opinion carries weight. Even though he doesn't think he is selling, the net result is that people buy.

The fear of commitment

I suppose one reason that many people think they don't know how to sell is that they're not particularly comfortable asking for the order. They have no problem presenting their case to a customer. But pressing that customer to make a commitment is an entirely different order of assertiveness. It's intrusive. It means drawing a line and asking the customer to cross it. It means risking rejection, which many people can't face.

In our company, I think we've solved that problem, although it was a costly lesson.

A few years back we hired a famous athlete for our television division. Here, we thought, was the perfect person to sell sports programming. He understood sports. He knew television. He had such prestige that he could get through to any decision maker. The only problem was that he was physically incapable of asking people to buy. He couldn't ask for the order. He couldn't close a sale.

In hindsight, I realize now that we could have turned this ex-athlete into an effective salesman with one small adjustment. We should have teamed him up with a 'closer', a colleague who could ask for the order.

Don't Tell Them When You Can Show Them

There are two ways to convince people that your idea is valuable. You can tell them about it, or you can show them. Telling them, no matter how eloquently you express it, comes down to making a sales pitch, and sales pitches tend to put people on guard. They feel they're being 'sold'.

Showing people what your idea can do for them makes them more receptive. They feel they are getting a no-obligation opportunity to assess your style and your level of competence.

In order to show people what you can do for them, however, you have to develop a canny sense of what they want. What people really want is not always what they appear to want or say they want. What you can really do for them is not necessarily at the heart of your idea as *you* see it.

I got an inkling of this paradox at the start of my relationship with Arnold Palmer. Arnold was skeptical about having a manager. He didn't understand why he needed another human being (namely, me) complicating his seemingly idyllic life. Furthermore, he didn't see any overwhelming reason why he had to share a percentage of his livelihood (namely, my commission) with that individual. Arnold's skepticism was well-founded. The idea of a golfer having a day-to-day manager was a novelty at the time. There wasn't a large market for golfer's services off the course, and even if there were a market, it had never been proven that a business manager could do a professional golfer one bit of good exploiting that miniscule market.

Arnold and I held a number of preliminary conversations while I was still a practising attorney in Cleveland, Ohio. I gave him my take on the opportunities I saw on the horizon – the endorsements, the licensing deals, the personal appearances that are taken for granted today but were nonexistent at the time. Arnold listened politely but remained aloof and noncommittal.

What I failed to realize was that Palmer was not primarily money-motivated. Through the years, he has become an extraordinarily savvy businessman – with ventures ranging from golf course design and management to aviation companies to automobile dealerships.

But it has always been the accomplishment, not the money, that motivated Arnold. Back in 1960 his sense of accomplishment was focused particularly and virtually without distraction on playing golf better than anyone else. If he did that, he expected everything else to fall in place. He didn't really know what that 'everything else' might be. That might be my job – if only I could prove it to him.

After several of these meandering meetings, it finally dawned on me that what Arnold really wanted was not someone to help him make a pile of money, but rather someone to help simplify his life so that he could concentrate on golf.

My challenge was to show him that I was that individual. I got my chance one night at the Palmer home in Latrobe, Pennsylvania, where Arnold, his wife Winnie, and I just had dinner. Arnold and I went into his study where he motioned in despair toward his desk, which was covered with a mountain of unopened mail.

'That's what drives me crazy,' he said. 'That's what I come home to after every tournament.'

Arnold and I continued our discussions, but I was barely paying attention. I was just biding my time until he got tired and announced that he was going to bed.

After he turned in, I attacked his desk. I spent half the night going through hundreds of pieces of mail, everything from fan letters to charity requests to supermarket circulars to business proposals.

The next morning Arnold woke up to a neat, nearly bare desk, with only three short stacks of correspondence for his attention.

'Arnold,' I said, 'forget the money. This is what professional management can do for you.' This is what he really wanted: simplicity, organization, peace of mind.

In hindsight, considering that I owe all my subsequent business success to my relationship with Arnold Palmer, this was the most important 'sale' of my life, and I did it by show rather than tell.

Handling Acceptance and Rejection With Style

How a salesperson handles acceptance or rejection says a lot about his future in sales. You would think that acceptance – i.e., a customer saying 'Yes, I'll buy your product' – would be the easiest thing in the world for salespeople to handle. But some people can't resist taking risks with their good fortune.

I've always thought that the riskiest part of a sale is the

moment when the customer says 'yes'. In many cases that's the instant when both customer and salesperson are elated that they've done a deal. But I suspect in an equal number of cases buyer and seller have totally different feelings at that instant. The buyer is *nervous* about what he's just committed to. The seller is *elated* that he's closed a sale. That's a dangerous emotional mix.

At that moment, it's imperative that the salesperson handle acceptance with style. In other words, once you've sold, shut up! Don't praise the buyer for having the good judgment to buy from you. Phrases such as, 'You won't regret this' or 'This is the best deal you've ever made', will raise suspicions in even the most trusting person. In a nervous customer, such phrases may change his mind.

Once you've made the sale, anything else you say about it can only work against you. So change the subject. Talk about the buyer's children or golf game, anything but how brilliant he is for buying your product.

If handling acceptance well means switching from the professional to the personal, then handling rejection well means maintaining your professional poise and avoiding anything personal.

As a general rule, you should never resent your prospects because they say no to your proposal. In most cases, they are rejecting your proposal, not you.

This is so obvious. Yet how often have you seen salesmen react to rejection by blaming the prospect – for wasting their time or being a jerk or not having the brains to recognize a great deal? They take it personally; they get defensive.

In extreme cases, this defensive attitude can become truly offensive, with salespeople lashing out face to face with prospects, as if trying to insult or intimidate prospects will somehow change their mind.

I approach rejection more calmly, even if I'm not feeling particularly calm. I'll go back to a potential client with another proposal and yet another. I'll do all sorts of things – send them newspaper clips, personal notes, invitations to events – to let them know that I value them, that there are no hard feelings, and that I still think we can do business together.

After spending so much time getting to know a potential customer, I'd be foolish to take his first or second or third 'no' as a cue to cross him out of my life permanently. The way I see it, as the customer's 'no's' accumulate, my odds of getting a 'yes' increase.

Chapter 6
For Sales Managers Only

Are Your Salespeople Being Proactive or Reactive?

As a manager I'm always delighted when one of our people reports on a big success that he or she has masterminded. Like anyone else, I love hearing good news.

But there's a part of me that's constantly analyzing these reported successes. How brilliant are they? Did they happen because someone in our company initiated the idea and brought it to life over tremendous opposition? Or did someone approach us with the idea and we just happened to answer the phone? In other words, were we being proactive or reactive?

The distinction between proactive and reactive behavior has always been important to me. It's not too hard to figure out why. Proactive selling – where you create the concepts, find the customers, educate them about their needs, and turn their buying habits upside down – means you're ahead of the field, a leader rather than a follower. If you do it correctly, you will always have first crack at the best clients, customers, concepts, and opportunities – because people will know that you are always bringing a little something extra to the table, a little more imagination or courage or aggressiveness. For that reason alone they will want to do business with you.

Reactive selling – where you merely respond to other people's ideas or imitate your competition – means you are an order taker. You are on the dull side of the cutting edge. You can prosper with this approach, but your business will always be at the mercy of someone else's initiative.

You'd think that everyone would want to be proactive rather than reactive. But the world doesn't always let you. Sometimes you can get trapped in situations that smother your proactive instincts – before you even realize it. Three scenarios to consider:

1 Early success

The most dangerous situation is having too much success early on – because it makes you arrogant and careless. I learned this first-hand in my early years with Arnold Palmer, Gary Player, and Jack Nicklaus. Golf was booming in the U.S. and our company represented the three best players in the world. It was an exciting time. The phones were always ringing. I was traveling around the world. Customers were literally walking into our office in Cleveland and suggesting business deals. I'd quote a price. They'd accept. And then I would gently usher our latest customer to the door – so I could move on to the next opportunity.

Under those circumstances it would be almost understandable if we began to think of ourselves as supersalespeople and grew a little self-satisfied with our abilities.

But selling our client's services was not where we lost our proactive instinct. We lost it in the way we recruited new clients.

I always thought that, given the success we were having with Arnold, Gary, and Jack, it would be obvious to all the other professional golfers that we were the best company to manage their business affairs. So I waited for the golfers to come knocking on our door. They never came.

Eventually, I realized that if I wanted to sign up the new golf stars and build our company, I would have to go out on the tour and get to know the players (which is what other agents, following our lead, were actively doing). I learned that before a golfer could appreciate our negotiating skills, he had to like us as a friend. The result: I became more proactive as a friend.

2   The windfall

A slightly different situation, but no less dangerous, is the windfall success. In our business it happens when one of our athlete clients breaks through to the top of his or her sport. Suddenly, the whole world is clamoring for the athlete. That's when the executives in our company who represent the athlete may begin to think they are better than they really are.

I've always said that it doesn't take a genius to make millions for Bjorn Borg when he is the number one tennis player in the world. Any wet-behind-the-ears schoolkid could manage Borg in a reactive way – that is, answer the phone, take the customer's offer and maybe bump it up by 10 or 20 per cent. I'm almost more impressed with the $10,000 sale that took initiative and creativity in a new area than a $1 million sale that was a foregone conclusion. The smaller sale is proactive. It's charting new waters. Who knows what we will discover there for our other clients?

3 Demanding customers

Customers are another reason that salespeople become more reactive than proactive. Some customers, after you have sold them your product or service, make such demands on you to service the sale that they prevent you from doing what you do best – i.e. , making more sales.

It's an insidious process that even the most alert and aggressive salespeople can overlook.

For example, in our company we are heavily involved in the sale of television rights for sporting events around the world. We have represented the international TV rights for, among others, the National Football League, the National Hockey League, and the ATP men's tennis tour. With that track record, it's not unusual for the directors of an event that has never had any success with TV rights to come to us and ask us to represent the event. We then do a mind-boggling job selling the TV rights around the world, earning our client a lot of money.

Around this time, with the TV revenues streaming in, the event directors suddenly insert themselves into our sales process and our activities. They want to know everything the foreign networks are doing for them – and more. What networks are buying the TV rights? How do they promote the event on air? Who are the commercial sponsors? What are the advertising rates? How many viewers?

All of a sudden, our people, who had been selling aggressively and creatively for the client, are forced into becoming almost full-time 'clerks' to answer the client's questions. (I remember one client asking us for the TV ratings in Venezuela when the ratings may not even be available in Venezuela.)

When that happens a good sales manager knows that the pendulum has swung too far, that his sales team has shifted from being proactive to reactive – and that neither the sales force nor the customer will benefit from the change.

Keep these three scenarios in mind as you gauge the achievements of your salespeople. If they become cocky because of some quick successes, show them the areas where they have room for improvement. If they have some big sales fall into their lap, gently remind them that it was probably more luck than their skill (and you can't always count on luck). If they become consumed by the demands of one customer, find them an assistant who can handle the niggling details and send them back out on the street to sell.

A Checklist for the Perfect Sales Call: Before, During, and After

I think every sales manager should take the time to create a checklist of what his or her salespeople should be doing before, during, and after a sales call. The checklist may vary in length from industry to industry, but I doubt if the techniques and strategies wander too far from the following list which people in our company have been using for years.

Although the list is obviously geared to our efforts to sell corporate participation in sports, I think it applies in almost any initial sales call at any company.

Before the meeting

1. Research the company, its products, current advertising approaches, etc.

2. Do a 'store check.' Find out how the marketplace perceives their product or service.

3. Consult our company data bank.

4. Discuss your ideas with at least one other executive inside our company.

5. If the company is already involved with sports, discuss this involvement with the appropriate sports executive.

6. For major meetings, obtain an Annual Report.

7. Find out the company's advertising agency. Have we had any experience with them?

8. Do they have an outside public relations firm?

9. Are you meeting on a Corporate, Divisional, or Individual Product basis – i.e., with a staff executive, a line chief, or a brand manager? This bears heavily on the size of their budget. (The brand managers often have the biggest budgets.)

10. Is the client new to the company? Your best prospects are people who have just come on board or are about to leave.

11. Organize your 'leave behinds'. Always leave something.

12. Know the title of the person you are meeting and, therefore, their ability to make a decision.

13. Know in advance who will be attending.

14. Reconfirm the day before.

During the meeting

15. Upon arrival, check the reception area for a company newsletter, etc. This will give you further insight and background.

16. Speak personally to the client's secretary. Thank her.

17. When introduced, remember all first names.

18. If you aren't clear about titles or positions of those in the meeting, ask up front.

19. Don't ignore the quiet one in the corner and play up only to the boss.

20. Find a personal issue that you have in common with the client (hometown, school, hobby, friends, etc.) to 'humanize' the discussion. Before they'll buy from you, they have to like you and trust you.

21. Make sure everyone in the meeting knows our background and services. Begin with a three to four-minute overview. Then let them talk.

22. In telling our story, be humble. Don't give the impression that we only do 'big' deals.

23. Before selling what you came to sell, get them to tell you what they want to buy. Ask, 'How's your business going?' and alter your sales pitch accordingly.

24. Listen to the customer. Don't just pay 'ear' service.

25. After listening to the customer, don't blurt out a response. Take a minute to consider the timing and whether you can use it to your advantage.

26. Whenever possible, include one of our successful case histories or involvements with someone else in their industry. ('Oh, I remember when we were working with XYZ and they had a similar problem and we suggested. . . .')

27. Be prepared to switch the sales pitch to another concept or service. Know your alternatives in advance.

28. Squarely face, don't duck the question: 'How can I measure the results of this sports marketing promotion you're suggesting?' We have a lot of experience in showing companies how to measure results against objectives.

29. Be sincere.

30. Don't have all the answers. That's their role.

31. Don't take all the alotted time if you don't have to. They'll appreciate you even more.

32. If you don't know something – a date, a price, a name – say so. Then get back to them with the right answer tomorrow.

33. In pricing your proposal, think in terms of goods and services (barter) as well as cash.

34. Once you've sold something, shut up.

After the meeting

35. The next day have a thank-you letter in the mail that summarizes the discussion and mentions everyone at the meeting. Send copies to all involved. Without fail.

The Three Most Important Documents in a Salesperson's File

I've never met an effective sales executive who doesn't have a system for assessing (and improving) the performance of his salespeople.

Some have elaborate reporting procedures and keep a

tight rein on their sales force. They know how every penny is spent, and measure it against every penny earned.

Others have fairly loose systems. They keep a running tally in their mind, based on what their salespeople tell them, of who's selling well and who isn't. As long as the income exceeds the outgo at year's end, they're happy.

I know one sales manager who insists on weekly 'What I Heard' memos from all his salespeople. These are written summaries of all the industry information, promises, rumors, and suggestions the sales force has picked up during the week. He contends that it improves internal communication and forces people to listen more and talk less. Most important, it tells him if his salespeople are hearing what the customer is actually saying.

'You'd be surprised,' he explains, 'how four people can go to the same sales meeting and then write up four totally different "What I Heard" reports.' (Actually, I'm not surprised.)

My sales management system is simpler. I keep three forms of documentation in each salesperson's file.

Production, quotas, and prospects

The first, obviously, has to do with *production*. I need to know how much a person is, in fact, selling. I get this in the form of activity reports and regular updates on income projections.

The second document outlines *goals and quotas*. It's important that the salesperson knows what's expected of him or her. So I keep a goal memo in the file for if the two of us should ever disagree.

The third document (and my personal contribution to the genre) is the *'balls in the air'* memo.

I am constantly encouraging our people via memos to have more prospects than they can handle. If they have ten balls floating in the air, I want them to have 20. I don't care how many balls they drop along the way. I'm convinced that the more balls they have in the air, the greater their chances of catching one (or more).

My big reason for emphasizing more balls in the air, I suppose, is to counteract the pernicious structure of most sales organizations. They are hierarchies designed to reduce, not increase, a salesperson's universe of prospects.

Most sales managers will tell you that they're trying to build a sales team. Yet look at their organization and you'll find a structure that is singularly designed to defeat teamwork. That's because most sales forces are still organized along the principle of territoriality.

Each salesperson has his territory, his sacred list of accounts that he has either earned or inherited. In a competitive environment, he's trained to jealously guard these accounts. They are the source of his income and self-esteem. For a colleague to broach a new concept to one of his accounts, without his consent – no matter how appropriate or rewarding the idea may be – is considered poaching. It creates friction rather than harmony. It is not 'team play'.

I don't buy that. In fact, I think the opposite is true. I think a regular memo that encourages people to put more balls in the air – in effect, forcing people to share information, overlap accounts, and risk stepping on each other's toes once in a while – goes a long way to fostering teamwork rather than negating it. And it has the added benefit of increasing sales.

Of course, there's a right way and a wrong way to encourage people. For one thing, you have to consider their fear of failure.

There's a reason people tend to float one ball in the air rather than 20. One ball is easier to catch. One customer who says no is a lot less damaging to a salesperson's ego than 20 customers saying no. That's why salespeople so often attach themselves to one prospect and doggedly pursue that to a conclusion rather than take the same idea to 19 other customers. They think they have decreased their risk of failure. They think that one 'no' is less of a defeat than 20. As a manager, it's my job to let them know that failing – even failing miserably – is all right. It's certainly better than wasting time on a so-so prospect, fooling yourself into believing that you are still in the game.

A 'balls in the air' memo must do more than hint that a salesperson should be approaching more prospects. It must leave the salesperson no choice. It's the difference between the boss suggesting, 'Why don't you call on XYZ Corp.?' and saying, 'Joe Smith at XYZ Corp. is expecting your call.' You're more likely to do the latter.

A 'balls in the air' memo must also make the salesperson feel that it is still his deal, no matter how valuable the boss's contribution. You cannot underestimate how strongly people will resist an idea if they feel they will have to share credit for it.

One of our salespeople was recently talking to an insurance company about a project. As it happened, I knew at least three other insurance companies that would be very interested in the project. I could have offered to call those companies on his behalf. But I suspected he would resist that – because if any of my leads came through, he would no longer get the full aesthetic credit for the deal. He would have to share the glory with me.

We all know credit-conscious persons like that. But you have to manage them, not ignore them. You have to insinuate your suggestions without threatening them.

A 'balls in the air' memo lets you do that.

Instead of offering to call the three insurers myself, I suggested that he do it. That put him back in the loop and took me out. It was his deal again. But both of us won.

Say Goodbye to the Solo Salesperson

I've always thought that one of the big attractions of being a salesperson is that you get to work alone. You're independent. You're time is more or less your own. The people you have to answer to, besides your customers, can be kept to a bare minimum, often to just one sales manager. There's even a little sizzle attached to the calling; there's something fundamentally heroic about a salesperson venturing into the unknown with nothing but a sample case and coming back with orders.

Of course, there are other compelling reasons for selling solo. For a sales manager, there's no confusion about who gets the credit (or the commission) when one person is working on a particular sale. It also increases a sales manager's reach; if you have a sales force of ten, you can knock on more doors if you send all ten salespeople out alone than if you team them up. Customers also tend to like dealing one-on-one with a salesperson. There's an ease and intimacy to a one-to-one relationship, particularly a long-term one, and there's rarely any confusion about who promised this and who said that. Dealing one on one, you can usually shake hands on an agreement and know it will happen the way the two of you discussed it. Adding a third person to the mix injects another opinion, which can be divisive.

Despite all this, I've become a big advocate of pairing salespeople together rather than letting them fly solo. I'm not talking here about simply teaming up a new sales recruit with an experienced salesperson who will take him around to customers and teach him how the organization operates. Pairing experience with inexperience is an obvious combination – and highly recommended when new people have to 'learn the ropes' quickly.

Rather, I'm talking about being a little more shrewd about the way all of us as sales managers combine the various and seemingly disparate elements in our sales force.

The first rule for sales managers in this regard is: Step out of the way. A lot of salespeople make it easy for a sales manager to team them up. They do it themselves. They recognize complementary skills and qualities in a colleague and gravitate toward each other. Over the years I've quietly watched the most unlikely sales teams forming within our company – young with old, buttoned-up with flashy, creative with dull, funny with humorless, smooth with gruff. I'm not sure they consciously decide to work together; it's not as if they announce one day that they're a team. But despite their differing personalities and style, fate has put them together – and the combination clicks. They sell more together than apart. When that happens, I'd be a fool to interfere.

The second rule: Don't force people together unless you recognize a serious flaw in one that a partner can correct.

The true test for pairing partners creatively is whether the combination of one plus one adds up to more than two. Here are three of my favorite combinations:

1   The CEO and anyone else.

It used to be said on the tennis tour that the greatest doubles team in the world was John McEnroe and whoever happened to be his partner. McEnroe was so good he literally elevated his partner's game.

It's the same at most companies. The best sales team should be the CEO and whoever tags along.

In recent years, as my schedule gets more complicated, I always try to team up with at least one other executive on my sales calls. If I'm trying to sell something to a senior decision-maker, it's quite possible that I could do it on my own. But bringing a younger executive with me to the meeting provides more benefits to our company than if I went alone. Being seen with his CEO adds a little to his stature and credibility. Participating in senior-level meetings elevates his 'game' a little. And if, at some point in the meeting, I give him a chance to take over the discussion, particularly in an area where he knows more than anyone else in the room, that adds a little more to his credibility too.

The real benefit comes later though, on the second or third meetings, which if I've positioned the younger executive properly, don't require my attendance at all.

That's the best reason for any CEO to team up with a junior salesperson: It helps that salesperson sell better alone.

2   The superseller and the lawyer.

Bringing an attorney to a sales call always elevates the importance of the meeting. It means you are serious about the sale or have some concerns about the legal elements. It also tends to make people a little more careful about what they promise to do. In some cases with an outside attorney, it might even speed up the meeting, since people may be aware that the attorney's meter is running.

But the best reason to partner someone with an attorney is to check their more outrageous selling impulses. I learned this with one of our more gifted sales executives. He had great mental agility and tremendous verbal skills. Put him in a room with a sales prospect and he could spin out a spellbinding web of concepts and programs that would dazzle the prospect. Unfortunately, his brilliance and enthusiasm sometimes got the best of him – and he often promised more than we could possibly deliver. As a result, he sometimes spent more time untangling us from his promises than actually selling. The problem disappeared when we started sending a lawyer with him on major initial sales calls. It was a beautiful good cop/bad cop routine. Whenever he took off on one of his patented flights of fancy, our lawyer would be there to reel him in, reminding him, 'We can't do that.' Teaming him up with an attorney made him more effective because he spent more time selling than retracting promises.

3   Starters and closers.

There are some people whose biggest skill is getting the attention of the buyer. In a way, they are like carnival barkers; their job is to get customers to step inside the tent. They make a fine first impression because they have enough razzle dazzle to get through the initial meeting. But they tend to wear thinner and thinner with every subsequent meeting – because they lack substance and depth. They can write great headlines, but they can't write the text.

It's not too hard to spot this type of salesperson. You analyze his ratio of sales calls to actual deals and see that there's a lot more calling than closing going on. I can appreciate how some sales managers lose patience and ultimately let this type of person go.

But a truly effective manager will do something else. He'll realize that bringing customers into the tent is a valuable skill. And he'll team him up with a detail-oriented executive who can help him close more sales.

It's like managing a baseball team. You don't get rid of a starting pitcher who can only give you seven good innings each time out. You find a relief pitcher who can shut batters down for two innings. Neither pitcher is very good on his own. But together they achieve the desired result: You win.

How to Identify the Real Hero in a Sale

There are four people involved in every sale: someone to initiate it, someone to maintain it during negotiations, someone to close it, and someone to service it.

In the not-too-distant past these three functions were customarily handled by one person. You called him a salesman.

But in an era of increasing specialization, where even

small law firms have partners to bring in business, associates to service it, and litigators to handle it in court, I suppose it's inevitable that the selling process, too, has been subdivided.

There's nothing inherently wrong with this. But it can cause confusion about who is the real hero in a transaction.

Is it the person who opens the door or the one who closes it? Or is it the people who did all the spade work? With so many heroes, who gets the credit and how do you compensate them properly?

It's a thorny problem. In a service organization such as ours, where we're selling the company's general expertise rather than a product you can carry out the door, it's one reason we don't have a sales commission structure.

For one thing, we can live without the grief of split commissions. But more importantly, we don't want people getting 'territorial' at the company's expense.

People on commissions tend to fight for their commissions. They build a wall around 'their deal' and devote as much energy to keeping colleagues out as they do to bringing customers in.

This is human nature, I guess. When people are forced to compete, they focus more on their competition than on what they're doing.

It occurs even when you don't have a commission structure. Like other sales organizations, we have executives who insist on doing everything themselves. They want to be alone. They won't bring in a deal, or involve anyone else in it, until they have it totally wrapped up. They're afraid they won't get all the credit. I hate to think how many times they and the company would have been better off if they had asked for help and used some of the in-house talent available to them.

In building a sales organization, you have to fight that impulse all the time.

You have to force your people to say, 'I need help', – for the company's sake – and then make sure that help is forthcoming.

You have to show people, through recognition and reinforcement, that the person who places a two-minute call to keep a sale moving forward is contributing as much as the person who spent five months arranging the sale.

Lastly, you have to create a reward system that focuses less on the reward than on doing the job well. The more emphasis you place on a monetary reward, the more inclined people are to do the minimum to get it.

Chapter 7
Advanced Techniques

How to Win a 'Shootout'

A few months ago the executive committee of a major sporting event asked us if we were interested in becoming their marketing representatives – i.e., finding corporate sponsors for their event and selling the broadcast rights to television networks around the world.

This was great news. The event in question is a first-rate venue for corporate entertaining. It always attracts a large TV audience. It generates millions of dollars in revenue, a portion of which would filter down to us as our commission. It met all our criteria of what a blue-chip sporting event should be.

The bad news was that we weren't alone. The committee had found three other companies that were also interested in the assignment. We would have to compete for the business in what one of the committee members called a 'shootout'. The committee explained its needs, outlined the ground rules for the competition, gave us one month for research, and then invited the four companies to Washington, D.C. where each of us would have three hours to tell our story.

This shootout scenario happens all the time in business – whatever the industry. If you're in sales, at some point you will have to engage in open combat with your rivals to win over a customer.

It's inevitable – because the customers encourage it. They like looking at several options (it's good business). They like being courted and fussed over (it's flattering). They like the free ideas (it's cost-efficient). They probably like the momentary power of having someone hanging on their every word and their ultimate decision (it makes them feel godlike).

For the seller, a shootout is not always so pleasant. Preparing for it can be some of the most intense, exhilarating, and rewarding moments in business. It can also be incredibly frustrating and demoralizing. After weeks of non-stop work and doing the best you can, there's a good chance that you'll have nothing to show for it, that someone else will walk away with the prize.

We happened to come out on top in this particular case, in part because we used some simple tactics that can give any salesperson an edge over his or her competition.

1   Chemistry before credentials.

Credentials, of course, are important in any sales presentation. Telling people who you are and what you've done before is essential to establishing your credibility and worth. But this emphasis on credentials blinds people to an equally important factor, namely personal chemistry. Before they like your presentation, they have to like you.

The knee-jerk reaction at most companies going after a big account is to send in their big guns, usually the CEO and the top two or three executives, as if there is some inviolate symmetry between the size of an account and the rank of the people pitching for it. They fail to consider whether the big guns are the most qualified people to make the presentation or even if their personalities will mesh with the customer.

One look at the committee members – all smart, successful, plain-spoken aristocrats from the Deep South – and we knew that they were more likely to respond to a sales executive who could genuinely ooze Southern charm rather than a fast-talking East Coast type who could not. That's common sense, but it's amazing how often companies forget this.

2   Less is more.

The fewer people you send to a presentation the better chance you have of getting the customer to like you. You can send your ten best people to a presentation, nine of whom may do a wonderful job, but if the tenth person on your team messes up, by appearing careless or too arrogant or flashy, that's who the customer will focus on. You will be damned – and undone – by your weakest link.

In the case of the committee, we took this logic to an extreme. While all three of our competitors used at least three people for the presentation including the CEO and COO of each, we sent one senior sales executive from New York. This wasn't a bad move.

It may have been slightly brazen, but it was also honest. Here, we were saying, was the fellow who would be actually working on the account. We weren't going through the charade of sending our top brass to pitch the account (as our competitors had done) and then delegating the day-today activities to unseen minions. Customers can spot this ruse the moment you walk into the room.

More important, it gave our executive three hours alone in a room with the committee. Inevitably, they began to focus on him personally. When they said, 'Tell us a little about yourself,' he spent 20 minutes talking about his schooling, background, and experience. This went a long way to creating a bond between him and the committee. I doubt if the same discussion would have come up if we had sent a team of executives.

I've always said that the best meetings are one-on-one – because distractions and personality conflicts are kept to a minimum. One executive facing down a committee was as close to this ideal as we could come.

3 Focus on one idea.

The worst way to sell yourself in that first big meeting is to try to overwhelm the customer with a lot of concepts, as if that is a testament to your originality and depth. You'll only confuse the customer and complicate the issue at hand.

You certainly should try to dazzle the customer with what you have done in the past, but do this quickly. With our company's track record, we'd be foolish not to mention our work with the Nobel Foundation, the NFL, NHL, Itzhak Perlman, Wimbledon, Wayne Gretzky, Joe Montana . . . those are big names and well worth dropping. But dwelling on them is irritating.

Customers, I've found, get very impatient listening to salespeople brag about their triumphs. They want to hear what we can do for *them*, not what we've done for someone else.

It's a little like dining at a restaurant with a 60-page wine list. A smart sommellier will certainly show diners the wine list, to let them see how big and diverse and excellent it is. But he also knows that diners want him to quickly focus their attention on the wine that is most appropriate for their meal.

4 Don't knock the competition, unless you can knock them out.

No matter how you feel about your competition, don't make bad-mouthing them an integral part of your sales presentation. You never know how the customer will take it; your competitors may even be his friends.

The only time you can knock the competition is when they are guilty of egregious or dishonest behavior and you are certain that disclosing it will knock them out of the running. But resorting to generalizations such as 'They're not as good as they say they are' only makes you look mean-spirited and small – and will raise more doubts about you than your competition.

5 Use testimonials.

The best way to brag about yourself is to let other people do it for you – in the form of a reference or unsolicited testimonial.

In this particular case, we had done an outstanding job a few years before for a similar event. With very little prodding from us, the head of that event called the committee and told them about our performance.

I mention this point last, but in no way is it the least important. In fact, I'm told it's a big reason we won the assignment.

Agents of Influence Need to Be Influenced Too

In every sales situation, the ideal circumstance is you dealing one-on-one with the ultimate decision-maker. No outside agents of influence are allowed into the discussion to distract the two of you.

Unfortunately, it's hard to achieve this ideal condition. There are always middlemen, go-betweens, brokers, hangers-on, spouses, siblings, parents, advisers, colleagues, companions, counselors, lawyers, accountants, and consultants around who inject themselves into the discussion and somehow prevent you from getting something done.

How you choose to deal with that interloper, that outside agent of influence, says a lot about your eventual success as a salesperson and negotiator. The fact is, you can't always ignore or confront these interlopers. Sometimes agents of influence need to be influenced, too.

For example, in our client business it's extremely important to pay attention to the inter-relationships between husbands and wives. Not surprisingly, spouses are the most omnipresent and therefore the most powerful agents of influence in an athlete client's life. And, despite their best intentions, they inject themselves into deals and projects in a way that conflicts with our goals and sometimes their mate's best interests.

We once had a case where a husband who had been a long-time client married a woman who perceived she had some expertise in one aspect of our business. She suggested very forcefully to her husband that we were incorrect in how we handled one of his broadcasting deals. She proceeded to set him against us. We didn't think we were incorrect and had several discussions with him trying to settle the matter and come to some sort of compromise.

Eventually, he took me aside and said, 'This is really down to a point now where it's a matter of pride between me and my wife. I can't face her unless I get the redress I was originally seeking – even though I see your position and think you're probably right.'

Because he was a long-time client and we wanted to maintain his friendship – and because we could never recover his friendship if we were responsible in some way for messing up his marriage – we gave him the redress he wanted.

That's one way of dealing with outside agents of influence: Yield to them. Sometimes it's the simplest, most prudent course of action. But I don't recommend it across the board. Yield too often and eventually everyone will walk over you.

Nor do I recommend the opposite extreme: Attack them. So often in our business, when the young athlete starts to date the woman who has an influence of one kind or another over him – whether this involves business or investments or lifestyle or cars or drugs or what tournament he should play the third week in April – the normal impulse is to say to the client candidly, 'She doesn't know what she's talking about!' And the client may agree with you. 'Don't worry,' he says, 'I'll take care of it.'

But over time, as they get closer to one another and this new woman gains more and more influence, you have to monitor the relationship carefully. There will come a time when you cross the line. It's no longer acceptable for you to attack this woman, because the client feels compelled to defend her or, worse, he actually believes she is right. (Incidentally, this is not a sexist issue of women clouding men's judgment. On the contrary, husbands and boyfriends of women athletes tend to be much more intrusive than wives and girlfriends of male athletes.)

There is a third course of action that is much more effective: Influence the agent of influence. Incredibly, most people never consider this. They are so focused on the decision-maker that they forget how much the decision-maker values the opinions of the people on his or her periphery. Ignoring these peripheral people is a mistake. Paying attention to them is uncommon brilliance.

The first thing you have to understand is the concept of a coterie.

Most sports personalities at all levels have a coterie of people who have nothing better to do than to hang around and be associated with a star athlete. They adore the star, dine with the star, travel with the star – and eventually get put on the star's payroll to continue adoring, dining with, and traveling with the star. The stars like this arrangement. They like having someone around who worships them and does anything they say. If that hanger-on is always telling the star how great he is, it's only natural that the star will listen to him as well when he starts venturing opinions about the star's career and business affairs.

It's no different in other walks of life. Every decision-maker has a coterie, whether he is a politician or movie star or CEO or moderately successful executive. People in power tend to surround themselves with people who make them feel powerful. And these coterie members have influence.

The second thing you have to gauge is your level of access to the decision-maker. Is it greater or lesser than the people in his coterie?

The natural tendency when you find yourself competing with a coterie member is to try to eliminate or discredit that individual. That's all right if you have full time to spend on such a campaign, if you have more access to the personality than the hanger-on. But usually you don't. You are entering and exiting the personality's sphere of influence. The hanger-on is always there.

In business, it's comparable to dealing with a CEO whom you know well and who respects you. But the CEO has a Number 2 whom you regard as a fool. If you were always in the presence of the CEO, you could probably neutralize or eliminate that Number 2. But you're not there all the time. And the Number 2 is. Over time you will lose the battle for the heart and mind of the CEO, because every time you leave the CEO's presence, the Number 2 will be there arguing his case and dismantling yours. In that instance, you would be much better off trying to get the Number 2 on your side, even though you don't respect him and would prefer to eliminate him.

This is precisely the campaign one of our executives employed some years back when we asked him to take over the management of one of our major athlete clients. The athlete at first resisted this new executive, in large part because he thought we were foisting a second-stringer on him rather than one of our stars. The executive's task was to convince the athlete that he was as good if not better than his previous manager.

His approach was ingenious. Instead of wasting his time trying to break down the athlete's skepticism, he identified three people in the athlete's coterie (his wife and two boyhood friends) and went out of his way to demonstrate his competence to them. It took two years, but eventually with these three people constantly extolling our executive's virtues in the athlete's ear, the athlete began to believe it too. The relationship has thrived ever since.

Remember this influence-the-agents-of-influence approach whenever you have to persuade two or more people to accept your position. If you can convince one person, there's a good chance the others will follow too.

The most daring example of this approach I can recall was applied by the director of a men's tennis tournament on the West Coast. One of the big problems in putting on a tennis tournament is that it's easy to get top players to show up the first year if the prize money is attractive. It's tougher to get them to come back the next year. But you need the players to come back in order to establish a profile for the tournament and to win the loyalty of your customers.

The tournament director had a limited promotion budget – and he was in a quandary about how to spend it. He didn't have enough money to advertise effectively on television and in newspapers. Instead of wasting the money on advertising, he spent it all on entertaining the players' wives and friends, whom he wined, dined, and pampered throughout the week. At week's end when he asked a group of players if they would come back the next year, all the wives leaped up and assured him, 'There's no way we'd skip this tournament.'

It Doesn't Always Pay to Make Everything Look Easy

One of the interesting paradoxes of being in a personal services business, where you're basically selling your time and talent, is this: The more talent and ability you have, the the more you can charge for your services. Also, the more talent you have, the less time it takes you to get things done. You'd think that getting things done quickly and being paid a premium rate for that skill would be an ideal situation.

But just because you can make things happen easily and quickly for your customers doesn't mean they appreciate it or are willing to pay a premium for it. In fact, a lot of customers discount the value of a personal service that is so easily rendered. That's the paradox: If you can solve a customer's problem in a day where a less capable person would need three weeks to achieve the same end, in a rational world you could name your price – and the customer would pay it gladly. But it doesn't always work that way. Many customers place a higher value on your services if delivering those services appears to be difficult. They value effort more than efficiency. They don't want to pay unless they can see you sweat.

(I've seen this same sort of thinking in sports. The tennis champion Pete Sampras has such a graceful, economical style of play that allegedly 'knowledgeable' fans sometimes question his effort and desire to win. Sampras describes his apparent nonchalance this way: 'When I'm winning I look like a genius. When I'm losing, I look like I'm tanking.' No one who knows Sampras or saw his performance at the 1995 Australian Open would ever question his desire and heart. But people get deceived when they can't *see* the effort and strain.)

I'm sure we're all guilty of this sort of thinking. If there's something wrong with our car, we wouldn't balk at paying $1000 to a mechanic who spent three days tearing down the engine to fix the problem. But what if a considerably more talented mechanic could identify and fix the problem in 30 minutes? Would we still want to pay $1000, even though it's the same result?

A lot of businesses are not victimized by this peculiar customer attitude. If you run a mail-order business and always have the best merchandise in stock and can guarantee next-day delivery, customers will gladly pay a little extra for your product line. They don't care how much effort it takes to get the results. If your restaurant consistently delivers the best meal in town, people will line up to pay top dollar to dine there. They don't care that you wake up at 4 o'clock each morning to select the freshest fish at the market. As long as the food is great, your effort is not a material concern of your patrons.

It's different in a personal services business where all you're providing is advice. People somehow become very interested in how much effort you expend on their behalf. They discount all the talent and experience that makes your advice valuable and put a premium on how hard you seem to be trying. That's why in so many personal services businesses – such as the law or consulting – clients prefer to pay by the hour. That's also why lawyers go to such great lengths to maximize their billable hours.

After a while you learn the awful truth: *It doesn't pay to make everything you do look so easy.*

One way to combat this pernicious thinking, of course, is to make your job look tougher than it really is. I know there have been times when a customer has called me up with a problem and the solution was on the tip of my tongue. I've had to bite my tongue with certain customers because I know they wouldn't appreciate such a quick solution. I tell them that I'll get back to them. And then I wait a few days or weeks before giving them my advice – because I know that's the only way they'll attach any value to it. It's a silly routine but some customers force you into it.

A better way to deal with these sort of customers, of course, is to educate them about what they are actually paying for. Sometimes this type of lesson requires a little creativity.

Some years ago we were hired by the CEO of a company in San Antonio, Texas to create a sports event celebrating the centennial of the Alamo. The event had to meet the CEO's very specific marketing objectives and had to be sufficiently attractive to get on network television. We came up with a race featuring the world's greatest milers. When we presented the concept to the CEO, he asked for a breakdown of the costs.

The total cost was $200,000 – $150,000 to the network for the commercial time and $50,000 to us for getting the city, the sport's governing body, and the network to support the event.

The CEO challenged our executive about the $50,000 fee. 'Why do I need to pay you so much,' he asked. 'All you did was make three phone calls!'

Our executive took three quarters out of his pocket and slapped them on the table. Looking straight into the CEO's eyes, he said, 'Here's 75 cents. Save yourself $49,999.25. You make those three phone calls.'

If the CEO didn't place sufficient value on all the imagination and influence that went into our proposal before that meeting, he certainly did after our executive's stunt with the three quarters. He gladly paid us our fee.

Chapter 8
How Selling Has Changed
(and How It Never Will)

No matter how sophisticated we all get at the 'art' of persuading people to buy our product or service, selling will always be a function of:

- Finding a need.
- Knowing your product.
- Believing in your product.
- Seeing lots of people.
- Asking for the order.

It's hard to argue with that. Most salespeople have a technique or code that's basically a variation on these five themes. One salesperson may put more emphasis on researching his customers (i.e., finding a need). Another may knock on more doors than anyone else (seeing lots of people). Still another may be a master at closing the deal (asking for the order). But the code doesn't change.

But salespeople are deluding themselves if they don't periodically rethink their sales methods and even their core beliefs. Customers and buying habits change all the time. Salespeople should too.

I know in recent months I've noticed changes in the sports and corporate marketplace that have made me re-evaluate some of my core beliefs about managing a sales force.

For example, whenever we opened up a new office in a foreign country we followed two hard-and-fast rules:

(1) The first employee had to be a salesperson, because only a salesperson could bring in the revenue to justify the office.

(2) This salesperson should be a national, because he or she would know the language, the culture, the ins and outs of the local sports scene. A national would have a reputation and some professional standing in the country. Those attributes would be useful on day one of our new office.

We stuck to this principle over the years as we opened offices in non-English-speaking cities such as Milan, Paris, Brussels, Stockholm, Tokyo, Budapest, Munich, Barcelona, and so on. Each of those offices is run by a native citizen.

But the incredible changes in the global economy have made us rethink the principle of hiring only nationals. I noticed this in 1994 when I visited our new office in Buenos Aires, which was being run by an American executive named Vincent Burniske. Burniske wasn't the obvious choice, but we gave him the posting for several reasons. For one thing, he really wanted the job and said so in an impressive letter that put forth his case. To his credit, he had sales experience. He knew sports. He was comfortable in a foreign country, having spent a lot of time organizing events in exotic locations. He was well-versed on our company's various projects and properties. His only deficiencies were that he was not Argentinian and he did not speak Spanish. Ordinarily, these would be major disqualifiers, but it was hard to argue with his enthusiasm.

The interesting thing I learned in Buenos Aires is that Burniske's non-native status is actually working for rather than against him. From the moment he arrived, he committed himself to studying Spanish several hours a day. He also enthusiastically embraced the local culture. In doing so, he has actually endeared himself to local business people. In Argentina, they want to see that you are in love with their customs and culture. They want to see that you are there to stay, not just passing through. They want to see that you are struggling to learn their language (and they certainly prefer clumsy Spanish to the assumption that everyone speaks English).

That's one way selling has changed. In the global economy, where everyone can communicate easily and language and culture are no longer insurmountable obstacles, you can uproot someone, send him off to a foreign land, and he can be effective there.

The part that never changes, and applies whether you're a native or an outsider, is that you have to build relationships before you can sell. With his valiant efforts at 'going native', our man in Buenos Aires is doing just that. The sales will follow.

A more serious change I've noticed in selling, particularly in the sports marketplace, revolves around a major shift in the buying habits of our corporate customers. Companies are no longer dazzled by the features that come with our sports concepts. They only want to know the benefits. This change didn't happen overnight. We've seen it coming for years.

It used to be that when we sold an involvement in sports to a company, the unique features of a sports event were the biggest advantages we had. That was the whole point of using our form of non-traditional media. If you sponsored a golf tournament, you not only got your company's name attached to a national event but you got a hospitality tent at the event where you could entertain customers and friends. You got signs and banners on the course which would be visible on network television. You could use the event to raise money for charity. And by bringing a golf tournament to town, your company could be perceived as giving something back to the community.

Each of these features of a golf sponsorship had a value to a company, but they weren't expected to specifically drive more traffic through the sponsor's stores or sell more of the sponsor's products. For that, companies had traditional media. They could put commercials on television or place ads in newspapers and magazines.

For years we concentrated on selling these features of a sports sponsorship to the corporate community. If the president of a toothpaste company loved golf, we could show him how to get involved in golf in a big way. Then it would be up to him and his marketing experts to use that involvement to sell more toothpaste. We figured we knew sports. They knew toothpaste.

But times have changed. The lines between traditional and non-traditional media became more blurred each day. There are more and more commercial messages cluttering sports. All of this causes more confusion at the companies who use sports as a marketing vehicle. As a result, they need and expect more guidance from sellers like us. They're not as impressed by an event's features – the signs, the hospitality suites, the money for charity. They want us to show how the event provides a direct benefit to their business. They want a direct dollar-to-dollar return on their investment. It's no longer enough for us to help them get involved in a sport. We now have to help them make money from it.

This development obviously demands a change in how

we sell. We're no longer just selling to a customer. We're becoming partners with the customer. It's not enough to just show him our product line and let him choose. We have to show him how to get the most out of the product too.

The part that has changed is that the customer seems to demand this sort of partnership.

The part that never changes is that forging these partnerships will never hurt you. They are the essence of selling.

Chapter 9
What's Your Selling IQ?

Now let's see what you've learned. How would you deal with the following hypotheticals that cover some of the thornier situations in sales?

Not Bad, Just Badly Assigned

Q: You recently inherited three sizable accounts from a colleague who took early retirement. In six months you've lost one account and managed to shrink the other two by half. You're puzzled. You are one of the company's top salespeople (that's why you got the accounts in the first place) and all your other accounts are growing. Have you lost your touch?

A: You're not a bad salesman. You've been badly assigned. You lack whatever chemistry existed between your predecessor and his customers. That's not your fault. It's your sales manager's for not realizing it. Ask for a reassignment before you do more damage to your company, your customers, and your career.

Going or Gone at Auction

Q: Whenever possible, you like to set up an auction atmosphere between competitors bidding for your product. That insures you get a more-than-fair price. Is there any downside to doing this?

A: For one thing, you have to watch out for collusion among the bidders. Even the most feverish competitors will balk when they think the bidding is self-destructive. That's when they may gang up on you. Despite regulatory restraints in many countries, you can sense when companies conspire not to exceed a certain price or take a hands-off approach to selected properties. It's difficult to prove these tacit agreements.

A more obvious danger: You can only go back so many times to the same bidder for more money before angering him. A sale at the maximum price is not worth it if it means losing a long-term customer. In such cases, we try to throw in a new ingredient – a longer contract, additional services, more time commitments from an athlete client, etc. This gives the bidder the feeling that he's getting more value for paying more. Better yet, it can escalate into a new round of bidding.

How Long Does a Sale Take?

Q: You've been working six months on a big account. After ten meetings with the customer, you still haven't closed the sale. Your boss is getting impatient. At what point do you give up? How long should the average sales process take?

A: Theoretically, you need at least three meetings with a customer to make a sale – the first to educate yourself about the customer, the second to educate the customer about you, the third to state your case to the person who can make a commitment. (Whenever we've made a quick sale, it's because we've done business with the customer before, our concept is 'hot,' or we got lucky.)

In reality, of course, successful sales require more than three meetings. Given the fact that many meetings are 'hunting expeditions' – where you're actually refining your pitch as you search for the appropriate decision-maker – your six months and ten meetings are not out of line. The real question you should be asking is: Are we making progress with each meeting? Are we advancing and refining the concept to a more receptive audience? Are we closer to closing?

The longest sale I ever made took eight years. For the first seven years I had no idea what to sell this major multinational company – and I didn't force the issue. But the more I got to know about them, the more convinced I was that we should be working together. And with each passing year, they came to believe that too. Finally, in Year Eight we came up with a golf concept that was perfect for them – and they bought it.

This tells me two things about lengthy sales: (1) We didn't know enough about the customer in the first seven years to come up with the concept. (2) If we had proposed the idea earlier, the customer wouldn't have known enough about us to commit to it.

Your Place or Theirs?

Q: You have an important meeting coming up and can't decide whether to insist the other side come to your office or to lose face and go to theirs. How do you decide whose turf to deal on? Does it matter?

A: Yes, it matters. But not for any reason of saving or losing face. At the CEO level – or any level for that matter – deciding on 'your place or mine' is usually a matter of convenience. For practical reasons, I try to hold as many meetings as possible in my office – because it saves me so much time.

The most important factor in choosing the site is not the 'power' statement it makes (whatever that means!) but the impression it creates. After years of going to people and having them come to me, I've discovered an interesting paradox: The more important they are, the easier it is to ask them to come to me. The less important they are, the more impressive it is if I go to them.

If you're really troubled by this, choose a neutral site such as a restaurant or private club.

The One-Shot Deal

Q: You know that many extenuating factors go into establishing the right price for a product or service, e.g., what the competition is up to, whether you plan to do business with the client in the future, etc. But how do you get the best price in a one-shot deal?

A: I never look at a sale as a one-shot deal. Every sale is the start of a lifetime relationship. Obviously, it doesn't always work out that way – but it doesn't hurt to think so in the beginning.

Giving Money Back

Q: You've received an overpayment of $85,000 from one of your regular (and, ironically, most dilatory) customers. You returned the check immediately to the customer and told your boss. You thought he'd get a chuckle that this habitually delinquent customer was suddenly paying too much too soon. Instead, he chastised you for not cashing the check and using it as a credit against the next time the customer was slow to pay. Did you do the right thing?

A: The short answer is yes, you did the right thing. But that doesn't mean your boss is necessarily wrong.

If you insist on seeing the overpayment as a moral issue – as if a stranger walking in front of you has dropped a $20 bill and you debate whether to pocket the money or return it – you should always send the check back. But the customer's habitual delinquency complicates the issue. That makes it a business decision as well. The customer is not a stranger. He's someone you know well. He's also someone who has, in effect, been borrowing from you interest-free. His pattern of slow payments means he has the use of your money and you don't. In effect, he has kidnapped your cash flow. I can see how any boss might justify keeping the $85,000 check as payback for all the times the customer kept you waiting.

I have canvassed friends about this sort of problem and the consensus is that the correct response depends on the customer's character and behavior. One executive told me that he immediately returned a recent overpayment because he didn't want the customer to use it as an excuse – no matter how contrived or bogus – for reneging on a deal point. The customer, in this case, is extremely contentious and litigious. Although the relationship remains smooth, this executive was thinking long-term. All sorts of things could go wrong in the future, but he wasn't going to let it be his failure to return a wrong check.

In most cases, the decision to return the check is a simple matter of honesty. But sometimes it's a question of efficiency or showmanship.

One woman who owns her own small business told me she has two clients who, because of their antiquated duplicate accounting methods, regularly (and annoyingly) double-pay her monthly retainer. This has been going on for years. In the beginning she sent the checks back to each client, along with a personal letter. She figured it was the right thing to do and she might get some vague psychological credit for being honest and buttoned up. But after a year of this, she realized it wasn't her problem. It was theirs. They had to get their acts together. Now she keeps the money and reconciles at the end of the year.

I remember some years ago when our television division comptroller received a rights fee from a central African TV channel. The check should have been for $1600 but a misplaced decimal turned it into $160,000. I remember he felt incredibly proud for getting on the phone immediately to central Africa and pointing out the error to the channel, as if he had done a deed worthy of sainthood. But I must admit a part of me was thinking, 'I wish he were as quick at collecting money we were owed as he was at giving it back.' Speed on behalf of our company rather than for someone else would have been more impressive.

If you're going to make a big deal out of returning a check, at least do it with some flair that extracts the maximum benefit out of the gesture.

One of our licensing executives told me he once received a $300,000 royalty overpayment from one of his licensees. He could have returned it immediately but thought better of it when he considered the check's full implications. In our licensing business, where we have dozens of licensing contracts in all parts of the globe and receive a steady flow of royalty checks on a quarterly or semi-annual basis, a frequent bone of contention between us and the licensees is the accuracy of their royalty statements. We often have to audit the licensees' books to make sure our clients are getting their fair share of the revenues from goods that bear their names or images. In our experience, licensees don't overpay. They almost expect us to challenge the size of their royalty payments.

Given this history, our executive decided to have some fun with the $300,000 check. He kept it for a few months until the next big meeting with the licensee. At the point in the meeting where revenues were reviewed – precisely where licensees expect us to raise the most objections – our executive made a big show of explaining that, after carefully totalling up our client's fees, we believed they were grossly misstated. 'They're so wide of the mark,' he said, 'that we demand an immediate correction.' That's when he pulled out the $300,000 check and turned it over to the licensee.

The licensee was shocked at first, then relieved. I have to believe our executive's dramatic flourish made a point about our integrity that had far greater impact than simply sending the check back the day it came in.

My point is, before you return the check, consider all the facets of your relationship with the other party. There's a routine way to do the right thing and there are clever alternatives that you and the other party will never forget.

Playing Hard to Get

Q: For months you have been bombarding a prospect with proposals to convince him to hire your company. He hasn't said no. But the harder you try the less likely it seems he'll say yes. What's your next move?

A: There's nothing more exasperating than the 'maybe' prospect. At least a definite 'no' lets you move on to better things.

Ask yourself if this prospect is the kind who means no but can't bring himself to say it. Better yet, ask him.

If he denies it, ask him to put himself in your shoes: How would he try to sell to himself? When prospects play hard to get, they usually have something specific in mind. Stop wasting your time guessing his secret. Persuade him to share it.

The Paradox of Big

Q: What would you do differently selling to a small company rather than a large corporation?

A: Flip-flop your preconceptions.

I've found that small companies are often very willing to buy my big ideas whereas large corporations often prefer my small ones.

That's because senior executives at giant companies tend to have far less decision-making authority than you expect, whereas junior executives at small aggressive companies usually have far more discretionary power than you imagine.

Once you accept this paradox, it's easy to reprioritize your prospect list – with smaller companies at the top.

Another point: If getting to the right person is the toughest part of selling, you'll have a smoother time in a small company – where the person who can help you is, at most, one or two doors away. In a large company, I'm frequently dismayed to learn that the right decision-maker is either in another part of the world or can't be found.

Rejection vs. Resentment

Q: You know in your mind that rejection comes with the territory in selling. But that hasn't made it easier to accept. What's the most important element in handling rejection?

A: Never resent your prospects because they say no to your proposal. In most cases, they are rejecting your proposal, not you.

This is so obvious. Yet how often have you seen salesmen react to rejection by blaming the prospect – for wasting their time or being a jerk or not having the brains to recognize a great deal? They take it personally; they get defensive.

I approach rejection more calmly, even if I'm not feeling

particularly calm. I'll go back to a potential client with another proposal and yet another. I'll do all sorts of things – send them newspaper clips, personal notes, invitations to events to let them know that I value them, that there's no hard feelings, and that I still think we can do business together.

After spending so much time getting to know a potential client, I'd be foolish to take his first or second or third 'no' as a cue to cross him out of my life permanently. The way I see it, as the client's 'nos' accumulate, my odds of getting a 'yes' increase.

Reach Should Always Exceed Grasp

Q: You try to set realistic goals for yourself and your employees. There's nothing more frustrating than pursuing unreasonable and unachievable targets. But it seems to be stalling your company's growth. By the twelfth month of the fiscal year, your salespeople are rushing around to meet their quotas but they rarely exceed them. How do you motivate the salespeople to be more productive?

A: Double their quotas. You might be surprised at how profitable things get even when people fall 10, 20, or 30 per cent short of the newly doubled budget. You might also be surprised at how employees – because of pride or fear or a combination of the two – will raise the level of their game to meet your expectations. In a well-run business, quotas tend to be self-fulfilling prophecies. Your people have already demonstrated they can do what you ask. Why cheat yourself and them with your rigid idea of what's 'realistic'? Set the bar higher and watch them jump higher.

A Cure for Debtors

Q: What do you do when a customer won't pay their bills? One of your biggest accounts repeatedly stalls on your invoices, which clearly require payment in full within 30 days. Then after three or four months of not paying, he wants to renegotiate the terms. Is it better to take a tough stance with this account, or cut your losses and get paid as much as you can get?

A: First, it should seriously bother you that this account is 'repeatedly' delinquent. That means you continue dealing with them even though you disapprove of their payment practices. Your first step is to cut them off until their account is paid up.

As for renegotiating payment terms, that may work with banks and third-world debtor nations, but you're not in the banking business.

You shouldn't be extending credit to customers who, by their actions, have bankrupted their credibility. Besides, what makes you think a customer who can't pay the full bill will be any more forthcoming when you cut the bill in half? (If you must renegotiate, at least get some leverage by insisting on a certified check before the discussions begin as a sign of their good faith.)

Take a tough stand. Don't get personally involved. Let your accountants and lawyers be the heavies. Be guided by the take-no-prisoners approach of George S. Kaufman, the American playwright and producer, when he confronted a theater owner who had mounted a Kaufman play without paying royalties.

'It's only a small, insignificant theater,' explained the producer.

'Then you'll go to a small, insignificant jail,' replied Kaufman.

Blind Letters and Cold Calls

Q: Your business frequently requires you to call executives at major companies about your product line. In most cases, your call has been preceded by a letter and product sample. Is it poor salesmanship to wait for them to call you, assuming that if they don't call they're not interested? When is the best time for you to follow up?

A: This is the problem built in to all blind letters and cold calls: You never know who's getting your message or even if you've gotten through.

Here's where your prospect's secretary can be your biggest ally.

First, call her to make sure her boss has received the material and looked at it. This is a familiar pretext for any follow-up call, but it works. Also, ask point blank if her boss is the appropriate person. If not, she may steer you to the right office.

Second, do not hang up without trying to set up a firm time to talk to her boss.

Third, never negotiate about the time. Call at the boss's convenience, no matter how inconvenient it may be for you. If you (a) politely ask, 'When is the best time for your boss?' and (b) point out that you only need two or three minutes to present your case, the secretary will usually set you up.

The Jekyll-and-Hyde Sale

Q: You've just met with a magazine publisher and her marketing chief to get their support for a proposed project. During the first hour, they raved about the concept, telling you they've heard similar ideas before but this was the first one worth pursuing. The second hour was grim. The publisher worried out loud about minor details and potential conflicts, asking you how you would solve them. How would you interpret this Jekyll-and-Hyde sales call?

A: Sounds to me like you made a sale – but don't realize it. Although it's important that you address the publisher's concerns about the minor details, you haven't registered the major detail that she likes your proposal.

Selling is tough enough as it is. Don't complicate it by ignoring the customer's positive remarks.

Of course, this isn't really a Jekyll-and-Hyde situation, since highs and lows within a meeting are standard procedure for most successful sales. After you resolve the big issue that you want to do business together, what else is there but to make sure that the small details don't tear you apart?

Handling a Sales Slump

Q: One of your star salespeople is suffering a severe slump. How do you motivate him?

A: There are all sorts of reasons why a super salesperson suddenly forgets how to sell. It happens to the best of us, usually when we forget the 'basics'.

When great athletes go into a slump, they always step back and re-examine the basics of their game. A golfer, for example, will break down his grip, his stance, his posture, and the various parts of his swing to get back on track.

The same thing happens in business. In as constructive a way as possible, you have to force your salesman to step back and reconsider some of the fundamentals that made him successful.

Is he spending too much time servicing existing clients, at the expense of finding new ones?

Has he fallen in love with the process of selling – the meetings, the proposals, the expense-account lunches – rather than the act of taking the order?

Has he lost faith in what he's selling?

Does he still know who his clients should be?

If you and he together can break down his methods to identify what he's doing wrong, it shouldn't be too hard to correct it and build him back up to where he belongs.

Hand Over Your Big Accounts

Q: You run a successful sales organization but still have to personally handle nearly all your major accounts. You're the one who originally sold them on your company and they still are only willing to buy from you. How do you wean the accounts away from you so you can concentrate on new business?

A: I used to wonder why our company didn't have more consulting arrangements with corporations. It was a profitable area and took advantage of our unique expertise in sports. For an annual retainer, we could review a corporation's activities in sports and recommend what else they should be doing or if they should be doing it at all.

It was actually an easy service for me to sell in a meeting with a chief executive whose company was heavily involved in sports sponsorship. If a CEO had questions about the effectiveness of the investment, I'd say, 'Let us take a look at it and give you our thoughts. Here's what we usually get paid by other companies. If you're uncomfortable with that, we'll do it for nothing for three months. Then you can pay us what you think our advice is worth, including nothing.'

I couldn't understand why our other executives who were constantly calling on corporations couldn't do the same, until another CEO pointed out, 'Mark, a chief executive will only give a million-dollar consulting contract to another chief executive.'

The CEO's point was that there was no way a mid-level executive at our company could pull off a huge consulting deal, where all you're selling is 'talk'. Mid-level executives simply didn't have the stature to price their 'talk' at that top-tier rate, nor did they have the authority to say, 'Pay us what you think it's worth.' Only I could say that.

I can appreciate this. As a chief executive myself, I'd have a tough time writing a big check to someone considerably junior to myself in experience, status, and track record. I'd want them to be my peer or close to it.

Before you can get out of this trap, you have to start building up your associates so they have the stature your big accounts can accept.

First, bring them with you on sales calls. Introduce them in the most flattering terms possible. Then give them the flloor. If they consistently rise to the occasion and impress your customers, eventually no one will notice or mind when you quietly slip out of the equation.

Second, give your senior people more impressive titles. This is purely cosmetic, but it works. It capitalizes on the unwritten protocol that, for better or worse, dominates communications between organizations: CEOs only talk to CEOs; senior officers only talk to their senior officer counterparts; and junior executives gravitate to other junior executives.

Third, insist that your newly elevated salespeople start upgrading the quality of the prospects they call on. Set real targets for them to meet new people in senior positions each year. If you can afford it, give them the time and budget to execute this plan. Your goal isn't merely for them to take over your major accounts. You want them to start creating major accounts of their own.

Making a Virtue of Smallness

Q: Your two-year old company needs a big contract to break through into profitability. But every time you bid for a major job, you hear the same excuse: 'Sorry, we went with a bigger outfit.' How do you beat this rap when you are starting out?

A: In a word, overcompensate. If size is not your strength, then make a virtue of your smallness. Do you have a proprietary concept or skill that no one else can match? Are you faster than a big bureaucracy? Are you more responsive? Can you promise all your time to one client? Are you nicer?

If you can find one thing you are really good at and then

exploit it, people won't care about all the things you can't do.

Requesting Sales Leads

Q: Your boss says that if you can't sell something on a sales call, you should at least walk away with some new leads. What's the best method of seeking referrals on a sales call? Is it appropriate?

A: I don't know if its 'appropriate' but it's good business. The key, of course, is timing.

A customer who has just said no to your proposal is probably feeling a little guilty about rejecting you. That's the perfect moment to say, 'Well, if you can't buy my product or service now, can I ask you to do me a favor?' Few people will turn away someone who needs a favor. Fewer still will do so if they have already rejected you on another matter.

That's the moment to ask the prospect to suggest colleagues, friends, competitors, and strangers who might be interested in your product or service. Most people will be glad to help.

The Price Is Too High

Q: You've lost three job bids in a row because the customer said your price was too high. Your profit margin was shaved so low on each bid that you can't imagine how the winning bidder is making money on the sale. Should you cut prices to get the business, even if it means losing money?

A: There's only one compelling reason to sell your product or services at a loss: A guarantee that you'll make money with this customer on the next deal. Those guarantees (and the customers who give them) are very rare. The reality is, a customer who always looks for the lowest bid isn't likely to change later on. He's still going to expect a lowball bid from you on the next job – or look elsewhere.

The Czechs have a saying, 'Don't jump high in a low-ceilinged room.' You need to find better customers, the kind who want the best bid, not merely the lowest.

There's a Line Between Persistence and Annoying

Q: You sell office equipment. Your sales manager accuses you of not being persistent enough in calling back customers. She says you would close more sales if you made more follow-up calls. Every two months or so she goes through your prospect list and literally stands over your desk while you call to see if they've made a decision. Do you consider that being persistent or annoying?

A: It's a fine line. There are people who can call a customer five times a week without becoming a nuisance. Conversely, there are people who annoy customers if they call once a year. How do you explain the difference?

Simple: The ones who get away with it never call without having some morsel of information that inches the sale process forward. In other words, they never call without having something to say. It could be a price change, a new product introduction, a change in specifications, or news about what a rival is doing – but at least it's legitimate news. It's hard for prospects to be offended by this call, when you're offering them information rather than pressing for a decision.

The tenacious sales manager is half right. You can never be too persistent. But you're both making a terrible mistake if there's no purpose to each call other than asking the prospect to buy.

Improving Your 'Closing Average'

Q: Around your company, you have a reputation as a terrific developer of sales leads. You can sniff out prospective customers and figure out a way to get your foot in the door better than anyone. But you're not as good at closing the sale. In fact, your expenses show you're making too many sales calls compared with the number of deals you bring in. Other salespeople are doing just as well with half the number of calls. How do you improve your 'closing average'?

A: When people have trouble closing sales, it's usually because they are not paying attention at the end of the sales call. The nervous edge and heightened state of awareness that every salesperson feels at the start of the sales call have worn off. Having said what they came to say, many salespeople relax, leaving the buying decision solely up to the customer. Actually, at the end of a sales call the customer is sending out dozens of clues that you can't afford to ignore.

The most obvious clues are technical questions. 'How do

you make these computer chips?' 'What are your toleran-
ces on this part?' 'Will these garments shrink?' Your brain
should leap into action when prospects ask technical
questions. They're telling you they're ready to buy. They
need to know the answers. The more technical the
questions the closer the sale.

Money signals are also good news. Like technical
questions, queries about price, payment terms, payment
schedules, barter deals, volume discounts are another way
of saying, 'I'm ready to buy'. These money signals come at
the end of the meeting, when the buyer really needs to
know. Don't ignore them.

I would also keep an eye on touchy-feely signals. If a
man walks into an auto dealer's showroom, takes a car for
a drive, talks price, gets back into the car, fondling the
steering wheel, playing with the buttons, feeling the
leather upholstery, he's sending a message that he's
interested in the car. If he comes back a few days later and
goes through the same routine, it's a good bet he's ready to
buy and needs the gentlest of nudges.

It's no different in an office setting. If the customer keeps
examining the samples you brought or browsing through
your color brochure or gesturing to the documents on the
table, he's a lot more interested in your proposal than he's
letting on.

Another promising signal is what I call the guest
appearance. If the prospect suddenly picks up the phone
and asks a colleague to join your meeting, be especially
alert. If the prospect hasn't already asked you the tough
technical and price questions, this new outsider will.

Pay as much attention to these closing signals as you do
to setting up the meeting, and your 'closing average' will
improve.

Separating the Professional and Personal

Q: A big customer, who controls 20 per cent of your sales volume is throwing his weight around. At least once a month he expects you to entertain him and his people – usually at dinner and a sports event. The clear implication is that this is part of retaining his business. You're not sure which is more irritating, the expense or the fact that he takes it for granted that you will oblige. If you enjoyed these evenings, perhaps it wouldn't be so bad. But you'd rather be home with your family. How do you get this customer out of your life without losing his business?

A: This is the strongest argument I can think of for separating – or at least compartmentalizing – your professional and personal life that I can think of.

Somewhere along the way, your 'big customer' stopped regarding you as a business associate and more as a friend. I suspect you encouraged this at the start – when you were wining and dining him to get his business. Is it any wonder that he still expects to be wined and dined by you now that you have his business?

That's the charitable view of this situation – that the 'big customer' wants to be your friend. A less charitable view is that he's using you to subsidize his nights on the town. Either way, weaning yourself from the relationship is not impossible.

You could take yourself out of the equation simply by sending him tickets to use at his leisure.

You could add another person to the equation by bringing along an associate. Hopefully, if the customer and your associate get along, your associate can take over the relationship. After a few evenings like this, no one will notice or mind the fact that you are no longer present.

Ideally, of course, you should have established your personal equation with the customer early on. There's no doubt that developing relationships is an integral part of selling, but you have to define those relationships as narrowly as possible. Anything less can overwhelm you.

I tend to be ruthless about segregating my personal and business relationships. That may sound cold and calculating. But it's also very sane. It doesn't mean I don't enjoy the company of people I do business with or that they aren't my friends. I simply prefer that the people I dine with or invite to my home or visit on vacation are people who have no economic entanglements with me.

Each of us presents different facets of ourselves to different people. Your customers see you as a salesperson. Your staff see you as a boss. Your neighbors see you as a parent or a volunteer at the local church. The problems begin when people who deal with one facet of your life start intruding or making claims on the other facets.

This sort of thing even happens to our athlete clients. Some years ago we represented a baseball player who had a lucrative endorsement contract with an automobile company. The arrangement was fairly straightforward. For several hundred thousand dollars a year, the company got to use the athlete as its spokesperson and his likeness in advertising. The company also got five days of the athlete's time for photo sessions and personal appearances. It was a great deal. The company really admired the athlete and used him well in their advertising.

At some point, however, people at the auto company began to overestimate their relationship with the athlete. They thought that paying him several hundred thousand dollars a year gave them access to every facet of his life. One time they called his team for 65 playoff tickets. They let it be known that their investment in the athlete entitled them to a major discount on the tickets.

This was intrusive. They didn't appreciate the athlete's various facets. As his sponsor, they dealt with him as a personality. When they called his team, they were intruding on his day job, on the area of his life where he was basically a team employee. It took some time to explain the distinction to them, but they eventually saw the wisdom of staying in one area and out of the other.

It might be too late to let your 'big customer' know that he is dealing with one facet of your life, that of a salesperson. But you should certainly keep it in mind for future customers. Be ruthlessly clear about how far colleagues and customers can intrude into certain areas of your life. It may seem heartless at first, but as your career advances and your list of contacts grows, you will be glad you did.

Who Comes First?

Q: You are going through a boom period in your business, to the point where you don't have enough product to fill your customers' orders. Should your oldest customers get top priority in filling the orders or your new customers whom you don't want to lose to a competitor?

A: If you can't decide, let the customers decide. Offer everyone a price discount if they accept a delay in delivery. Some will take the discount. Some will insist on immediate delivery. But at least you won't be the one making the choice at random. The net effect: Your customers will be establishing your priority list – which is the way it should be.

Getting Calls Returned

Q: You can't get people to return your phone calls, even after three or four tries. You're not sure if they're really busy, really disorganized, or really rude. What's the secret to getting calls returned?

A. When all else fails, call a third party. Ask someone who has influence with the person you're trying to reach – it could be a boss, a friend, a relative – to intercede on your behalf. If the request comes from a boss or colleague, the individual will comply out of embarrassment; he doesn't want to look disorganized or unresponsive. If it comes from a relative or friend, most people will call back out of courtesy. Either way, you will make a connection.

Talk to the Customers Who Left

Q: As part of a massive drive to boost sales at your company, you have started surveying customers to find out what you're doing wrong and how you can improve. But your CEO hates anything that smacks of 'market research', especially when the results don't conform with his preconceived opinions. How do you turn him around?

A: If the boss hates research, don't call your survey 'market research'. Summarize your findings in a random list of

'What Our Customers Like' and 'What Our Customers Don't Like'.

But that's just labeling. The more serious problem is you're surveying the wrong people. Instead of talking to current customers who obviously like you if they're still buying from you, you should be talking to former customers – to find out why they left! They're the ones who'll give you the unvarnished truth.

In that sense, perhaps your CEO is not so silly to question your survey?

Rejected for the Wrong Reasons

Q: What do you do when a sales prospect rejects your proposal for a reason that makes no sense? A potential customer said he didn't want to buy your product because you used to do business – five years ago! – with one of his competitors. That excuse confounds me. Should you tell the customer he's stupid? Is it worth the effort?

A: Assuming that there is a genuine need for your product or service, buyers generally have three reasons for saying no to you:
- They don't like what you're selling.
- They don't have the money.
- They don't like you.

Buried somewhere within these categories is the reason the prospect said no. Your job is to determine which one applies to you.

If people don't like what you're selling – e.g., because they don't think it measures up in quality or reliability –

another sales call might convince them that they have misjudged you.

If they don't have the money, I doubt if another meeting will suddenly enrich them.

If they don't like you personally, it will take a lot more than one meeting to change their mind.

Keep in mind that a lot of people are uncomfortable saying no (it's much more pleasant to say yes) and that at least two of these reasons could be considered inflammatory. As a result, a lot of people go through incredible mental gymnastics to avoid a confrontation where they have to admit they don't like what you're selling or they don't like you. This is how the far-fetched excuse is sometimes born.

We all do it. If a boring neighbor invites you to his home for dinner and you don't want to go, you don't decline by telling him that you think he's a windbag and a bore. Who needs the confrontation? You say you're busy that night. If he persists with future invitations and you continue to say no, eventually he'll take the hint. Only if he becomes a pest will you tell him the truth.

Given this dynamic, the next move is up to you. If you politely go back to this customer, he may string you along for months – or you may make a sale. On the other hand, if you tell him he's stupid, that's confrontational. You won't make a sale, but you'll certainly find out the real reason you didn't.

The Delinquent Customer

Q: Several of your regular customers have become delinquent in paying their accounts. It's making you look bad with your sales manager, who's holding you responsible for collecting the money on your sale. How much latitude should you give a good customer who's falling behind on his debts? And how do you convince your boss to give your accounts more time?

A: There's a theory that if you don't have any bad debts you aren't selling enough. If the bad debts represent a small percentage of your sales volume – and 95 per cent of your accounts are paying on time – your sales manager should be more patient. If they're 50 per cent of your business, the urgency is justified.

They Can't Say No

Q: How do you cope with a sales prospect who never comes out and tells you yes or no? You've called the prospect every week for a decision but he always says to call back next week. You have too much time invested in the sale to give up now. How do you close the sale?

A: This reminds me of a celebrity reporter who explained to me that in Hollywood the movie stars never say no when you ask them for an interview. They say yes. Then when you call on Monday, they say to call again on Tuesday, then Wednesday, and so on for weeks. The only strategy that works is persistence. Eventually they gave in, often because they felt guilty about mistreating you.

In this case, fight fire with fire. Try calling the prospect every day for an answer instead of once a week. It might be obnoxious, but so is the prospect's behavior.

Index